How To Get FREE Money For College!

The Ultimate Guide To...

Sending Your Kids To The Best, Most Expensive Colleges In America For Pennies On The Dollar!

2nd Edition

Trevor Ramos

Printed in the United States of America

Ramos, Trevor
        How to get free money for college: the ultimate guide to sending your kids to the best, most expensive colleges in America for pennies on the dollar / Trevor Ramos —2nd ed.
        p.   cm.
        ISBN-13: 978-1508769828
        ISBN-10: 1508769826
        1.   Scholarships. 2. Grants. 3. Financial Aid

Attention: High Schools, Middle Schools, and Community Organizations: "How To Get Free Money For College!" is available at quantity discounts with bulk purchases for educational or business use. For more information, please contact Trevor Ramos at the phone number below.

Editor: Blade Thomas

Trevor Ramos
1055 E Colorado Blvd, Suite 500
Pasadena, CA 91106
Phone: (626) 657-7887
trevor@collegefundingremedies.com

To my mother,
Rose Arana-Sabala who
made countless sacrifices to
make sure I had a great
education growing up.

"Our progress as a nation can be no swifter than our progress in education. The human mind is our fundamental resource."

John F. Kennedy (1917- 1963)

Contents

Vital Note:

Every section and every chapter in this book is important and serves a purpose. However, what most parents want to know is "**How to Get the MONEY**."

That's why I put the money section first. In this recently updated section I guide you step-by-step on where the money is, and how to get it.

In reality, the money section should be the last part of this book. It is my best hope that once you read the money section, you will clearly understand why it is so important to follow all the other important steps, insights, and secrets that make it possible for you to be in a position to ask for a large sum of money and get it.

All the information in this book is designed to give you and your student a crystal clear view of what we are about to do and exactly how we will do it.

I promise the end result will be worth every minute of your time, effort, and energy. On average, my students get approximately $84,787 over 4 years in free money scholarships and grants to pay for college. Some get a little less and some get a lot more.

Whatever you do, stay the course and you will not only be surprised at how much money the colleges and universities are willing to give your student to attend, but you will also have a great sense of pride and excitement knowing how much cash you've saved yourself and your child for a great college education.

All the best,

Trevor Ramos

Certified College Planning Specialist

P.S.   If you have questions or concerns, I am only a phone call away. You can reach me directly at 626-657-7887. If the line is busy please try again, or leave a message and I will be sure to return your call.

1

Introduction

"A man who has never gone to school may steal from a freight car; but if he has a university education, he may steal the whole railroad."
— Theodore Roosevelt

If you have a child or children you want to go to college and get a good education so they can become successful in life, please read this book carefully. It contains information of a high-dollar value that can help pay for most (and maybe all) of the cost to send your kids to the top universities and colleges in America.

More specifically, if your kids are between the ages of 13 and 19 and you expect them to go to college, you are going to have to pay for their college education or, -- they will be forced to take out student loans that will take 10-25 years after graduation to pay off. *Student Loan Payments* will be the size of a mortgage payment – without the house!

Your children could, of course, get athletic scholarships, but in reality, the odds of a full ride athletic scholarship are similar to the chances of winning the lottery. What you really want is a sizeable scholarship or grant that can pay a huge chunk of tuition, room, and board. The scholarships and grants I'm talking about are free money that neither you nor your student will have to pay back.

It doesn't matter if you are making $100,000 per year or $1,000,000 per year. Once parents learn the techniques and strategies I reveal in this book, they feel a huge sigh of relief knowing they are not going to have to spend all their hard-earned money sending their kids to college.

Please let me explain. My name is Trevor Ramos. I am a graduate of Boston University and President of College Funding Remedies, a national leader in the provision of high-end college planning solutions to families across America.

My specialty is showing parents of college-bound high school students how to get free money to pay for their children's college education regardless of income, assets, or grades.

I am known for producing consistent and extraordinary results. I am also an absolute financial wizard with spreadsheets, financial statements, and financial aid applications for college funding.

Students and parents who complete my program receive between $4,000 to $58,481 per year (per student) in scholarships and grants to attend top American colleges and universities. Some get more; few get less. That means you can easily save $16,000 to $233,294 over 4 years per child by following my advice. It's like getting a bonus or a raise every year for the total amount of free money you get awarded each year your child is in college. That's a handsome six figure income!

My best publicity comes from referrals because when it comes to advertising and marketing, I am modest, soft spoken, and not into the "marketing-hype" media personalities turn to for attention. In fact, it is simply not my personality to tout, or be boastful about my own skills and accomplishments.

However, the students and families I've helped to get into the colleges of their dreams – and then to find the *financial aid* to pay for a first-class education –have no problem telling others how I found them money when there was none.

They have no problem telling others that I showed their parents how to preserve their retirement savings and to avoid blowing the equity they've built into their homes and businesses to pay for their kids' college.

For example, here's a letter I received from a divorced doctor finding a way to pay for her two (2) kids to attend top colleges.

To other parents

Re: Trevor Ramos

"I want to share my endorsement for the guidance you will receive from Trevor Ramos as you embark on finding a good college/university for your son or daughter.

I am a single mom with a unique situation. The economy and our family situation led me to move to a different state during my daughter's junior year of high school.

I allowed her to stay in our original state with friends and family to complete high school. It was the right decision for my daughter, but made the arduous task of helping my eldest child choose a college complicated. We could not have those casual conversations parents and kids have at the dinner table, or driving from one school event to the other.

It is really hard for a junior or early senior to think of the end of high school, and hence, my daughter and I were struggling with the topic.

As of October her senior year, she only had one school she was willing to apply to, and it was a stretch school for acceptance and a huge stretch for finances. That is when we enlisted help. We were assigned to Trevor for guidance. This is exactly what he offered:

He engaged my daughter in a meaningful dialogue of her wishes, her interests, her preferences and helped her draft a list of colleges/universities best suited to meet her desires. She studied the list and chose 7-8 colleges to apply to.

Trevor also knew as a single mom, that finances were certainly an issue. As he drafted the list of viable colleges/universities, he paid attention to which colleges/universities had a good track record of giving larger sums of financial aid and scholarships. This proved to be very important.

As we moved closer to college application deadlines, Trevor kept my daughter on track for getting letters of recommendations from her teachers, filling out the on-line applications and writing her essays. My daughter is one who leaves things to the deadline and for a while I was not sure she would finish her applications, but Trevor said to relax and that he knew she would, and she did! Sometimes on the last date, but she did get her applications sent in.

Now the next step of assistance from Trevor was truthfully priceless. My ex-husband and I still don't communicate with ease. I was anxious about matters both of us had to handle regarding FAFSA and CSS Profile for my daughter's well-being. Well, Trevor handled all of those conversations with my ex-husband. Each of us did our part, but without having to get into our usual difficult and awkward communications.

When the acceptances came in, and the financial packages arrived, Trevor helped us interpret them, as well as sit down and evaluate a 4- year plan of how to pay for the loans and other expenses.

Trevor made the experience much easier from a parenting point of view. I knew I was not alone navigating through a complex system of overwhelming and scary costs. I knew I was not left nudging and pushing my daughter in a direction she wanted, yet was having trouble seeing. She felt safer discussing these topics with a neutral and knowledgeable party. Lastly, he took strain out of handling financial forms with my ex-husband, and allowed us to really focus on my daughter.

My daughter did not get into the stretch school she had on her original list when she was only planning to apply to one college. Instead, she got into her FIRST choice college – Bard College in upstate New York - after being shown what was available to her. Between scholarship, and government loans we were awarded over $45,000 and able to borrow the rest of what we needed in Parent Direct Loans.

I visited the colleges my daughter was accepted at with her. When she visited Bard, she said to me "Mom, I believe this is where I can really rise to be my best me." She is at Bard College and has blown me away during her freshman year with her maturity, her writing, her great grades and handling all the transitions like a champ. She truly is becoming the best young woman I could ask for. My daughter will study Japanese in Japan this summer, and Bard once again, provided scholarship to make that happen.

I am so thankful for the guidance Trevor gave us: his confident and reassuring hand, his knowledge, and his ability to guide us to colleges that did have money to support my daughter's education.

Trevor has now met with my son, who is a sophomore in high school. We did not think of asking for guidance until late in my daughter's senior year, but there is so much more one can do if you begin your college planning earlier on. My son, who likes to study, and get good grades, may have access to more scholarships money by preparing for his PSAT in his junior year.

As a sophomore, I already hear him comparing colleges that he wants to attend and focusing on his future.

Thank you Trevor, from the bottom of my heart, for the guidance you have provided to me and both of my children."

– Karen

Over the past six years I have personally helped just over 200 families find the money to pay for all or a sizeable portion of college tuition and expenses.

For example, here are 10 students I've helped just this past year:

(**NOTE:** All student and parent names appearing in this work have been changed to fictitious names to protect the privacy of the families.)

- Abbey received $60,000 over 4 years in free money scholarships and grants to attend Simmons College in Boston, MA
- **Sabrina received $160,400 over 4 years in free money scholarships and grants to attend Boston College in Chestnut Hill, MA**
- Tara received $73,734 over 4 years in free money scholarships and grants to attend Claremont McKenna College in Claremont, CA
- **David received $129,336 over 4 years in free money scholarships and grants to attend University of California: Santa Barbara in Santa Barbara, CA**
- Iris received $144,740 over 4 years in free money scholarships and grants to attend University of Dallas in Irving, TX
- **Mallory received $129,436 over 4 years in free money scholarships and grants to attend Chapman University in Orange, CA**
- Rachel received $102,920 over 4 years in free money scholarships and grants to attend University of Hartford in West Hartford, CT
- **Eva received $60,580 over 4 years in free money scholarships and grants to attend University of California: San Diego in San Diego, CA**
- Johnny received $85,136 over 4 years in free money scholarships and grants to attend University of California: Riverside in Riverside, CA

- **Caroline received $224,224 over 4 years in free money scholarships and grants to attend University of Southern California in Los Angeles, CA**

The total in free money grants and scholarships for these 10 students is a whopping $1,170,506 over 4 years! It's also an average of $117,051 per child that never has to be paid back! That's $29,262.50 PER YEAR all in free money—no student loans included!

I'm proud of this number and I'm proud of my work. I'm also proud of each student who followed my game plan, saved their parents thousands of dollars and are on their way to getting the best education money can buy from the top colleges and universities in America.

In fact, here's the list of all the colleges I've gotten my students into and how much money we've gotten projected over 4 years:

College	Annual Grant and/or Scholarship	Projected Over 4 Years
Allegheny College	$31,065	$124,260
Arizona State University	$12,500	$50,000
Assumption College	$15,000	$60,000
Azusa Pacific University	$15,550	$62,200
Azusa Pacific University	$15,550	$62,200
Bard College	$39,050	$156,200
Baylor University	$16,600	$66,400
Boston College	$40,100	$160,400
Boston University	$30,000	$120,000
Boston University	$15,900	$63,600
Boston University	$51,145	$204,580
Boston University	$17,800	$71,200
Bradley University	$4,000	$16,000

California Lutheran University	$32,758	$131,032
California Lutheran University	$23,284	$93,136
California State University - Long Beach	$9,967	$39,868
Carroll College	$13,021	$52,084
Case Western Reserve University	$44,935	$179,740
Case Western Reserve University	$37,510	$150,040
Chapman University	$29,508	$118,032
Chapman University	$29,745	$118,980
Chapman University	$29,300	$117,200
Chapman University	$20,850	$83,400
Claremont McKenna College	$43,939	$175,756
Claremont McKenna College	$24,578	$98,312
Clark University	$20,145	$80,580
College of the Holy Cross	$5,550	$22,200
Dartmouth College	$29,844	$119,376
DePaul University	$15,000	$60,000
Dickinson College	$42,630	$170,520
Drexel University	$24,495	$97,980
Drew University	$36,645	$146,580
Evergreen State College	$11,500	$46,000
George Washington University	$30,000	$120,000
George Washington University	$45,245	$180,980
Gonzaga University	$18,070	$72,280
Graceland University	$10,000	$40,000
Green Mountain College	$32,050	$128,200
Hartwick College	$30,150	$120,600

Johns Hopkins University	$41,900	$167,600
Johnson & Wales University	$13,000	$52,000
Lewis & Clark College	$31,162	$124,648
Liberty University	$6,700	$26,800
Loyola University Chicago	$22,500	$90,000
Loyola University Chicago	$15,000	$60,000
Loyola Marymount University	$24,200	$96,800
Loyola Marymount University	$13,800	$55,200
Manhattan College	$13,500	$54,000
Marymount College	$26,008	$104,032
Marymount College	$20,000	$80,000
Marymount College	$20,500	$82,000
Menlo College	$18,700	$74,800
Mills College	$40,309	$161,236
Mississippi State University	$12,500	$50,000
New York University	$34,650	$138,600
Northeastern University	$15,000	$60,000
Northern Arizona University	$4,000	$16,000
Notre Dame De Namur University	$10,000	$40,000
Occidental College	$60,712	$242,848
Pace University	$12,000	$48,000
Pacific Lutheran University	$19,102	$76,408
Pacific Lutheran University	$21,000	$84,000
Pacific Lutheran University	$17,000	$68,000
Pacific Lutheran University	$20,166	$80,664
Pepperdine University	$21,896	$87,584
Point Loma Nazarene	$7,680	$30,720

Post University	$23,550	$94,200
Prescott College	$8,250	$33,000
Purdue University West Lafayette	$10,000	$40,000
University of Dallas	$12,000	$48,000
Santa Clara University	$55,735	$222,940
Santa Clara University	$58,481	$233,924
Seton Hall University	$22,500	$90,000
Seton Hall University	$14,500	$58,000
Seton Hall University	$17,095	$68,380
Simmons College	$15,000	$60,000
St. Johns University	$14,956	$59,824
St. Johns University	$12,500	$50,000
St. Johns University	$19,000	$76,000
St. Mary's College of California	$13,000	$52,000
St. Mary's College of California	$16,000	$64,000
SUNY College of Environmental Science and Forestry	$17,900	$71,600
Texas Christian University	$15,420	$61,680
The American Musical and Dramatic Academy	$11,500	$46,000
The Catholic University of America	$29,200	$116,800
Tulane University	$27,000	$108,000
Tulane University	$22,500	$90,000
Tulane University	$27,000	$108,000
Tulane University	$32,000	$128,000
Unity College	$16,820	$67,280
University of Alabama	$25,950	$103,800
University of Arizona	$4,500	$18,000
University of Arizona	$9,500	$38,000

University of California – Los Angeles	$9,081	$36,324
University of California - San Diego	$17,820	$71,280
University of California - San Diego	$8,129	$32,516
University of California - Santa Barbara	$23,730	$94,920
University of California - Santa Barbara	$22,617	$90,468
University of California - Santa Barbara	$23,810	$95,240
University of California - Davis	$23,523	$94,092
University of California - Davis	$19,055	$76,220
University of California - Irvine	$21,840	$87,360
University of California - Irvine	$7,543	$30,172
University of California - Irvine	$21,493	$85,972
University of California - Merced	$25,244	$100,976
University of California - Merced	$18,639	$74,556
University of California - Riverside	$9,870	$39,480
University of California - Riverside	$21,294	$85,176
University of Colorado-Boulder	$6,250	$25,000
University of Dallas	$19,000	$76,000
University of Dallas	$36,185	$144,740
University of Denver	$15,000	$60,000
University of Hartford	$21,000	$84,000
University of Hartford	$21,000	$84,000

University of Hartford	$25,730	$102,920
University of La Verne	$19,500	$78,000
University of La Verne	$11,000	$44,000
University of Miami	$10,000	$40,000
University of New Mexico	$17,085	$68,340
University of New Mexico	$15,337	$61,348
University of Oregon	$9,000	$36,000
University of Puget Sound	$20,700	$82,800
University of Puget Sound	$26,595	$106,380
University of Puget Sound	$11,595	$46,380
University of Puget Sound	$18,000	$72,000
University of Puget Sound	$16,000	$64,000
University of Redlands	$17,000	$68,000
University of San Diego	$12,850	$51,400
University of San Diego	$20,000	$80,000
University of San Francisco	$20,000	$80,000
University of Southern California	$30,000	$120,000
University of Southern California	$9,098	$36,392
University of Southern California	$30,892	$123,568
University of Southern California	$56,056	$224,224
University of the Pacific	$12,500	$50,000
University of the Pacific	$10,000	$40,000
University of the Pacific	$11,000	$44,000
University of the Pacific	$30,458	$121,832
University of the Sciences	$16,000	$64,000
Wentworth Institute of Technology	$10,500	$42,000
Westmont College	$22,848	$91,392
Wheelock College	$11,000	$44,000
Whittier College	$19,000	$76,000

Willamette University	$24,100	$96,400
Willamette University	$15,000	$60,000
Wheaton College	$15,000	$60,000
Xavier University	$9,000	$36,000
Total Free Money For College	**$3,112,937**	**$12,451,748**

The average award money listed here is $21,197 per year or $84,787 projected over four years. Median scholarship or grant listed here is $19,000 per year or $76,000 over 4 years.

Each time I look at the list of scholarship and grant offers and tally up how free scholarship and grant money I've help to attain from all these colleges over the years, it makes me realize what I do in a whole new light.

This is what makes America so great. These kids are the future of our country. College wasn't gifted to them by their parents.

They paid attention, focused, and did what was necessary to make sure they got thousands of dollars in financial aid that didn't come from their parents, and they won't have to pay back in student loans for 15-25 years after they graduate.

Sure, some of them will owe $10,000 to $35,000 in federal student loans if they opt for them, but that is far less than the in free money to attend their dream colleges.

Save Money & Teach Your Children A Valuable Money Lesson!

It's amazing when you think about it. This is a great opportunity to show your children how finally to earn the big money. In other words, when's the last time someone offered your teen $21,197 per year? It's also great way to teach your children about money and how to approach getting an advanced education without having to stomach the financial destruction of their parents or their future. It's a win for parents and a win for the students.

But this book is about more than helping you and your student(s) pay for college. Here is a letter I received from a student who attended a high-end private high school in southern California.

"Working with Trevor has been great. He has helped me throughout my entire college admissions process. Having Trevor as a college counselor has been more than just a bonus to my high school counselor, he is a necessary addition.

He has given me personal assistance with building a college profile, finding colleges that well suit my wants and needs, writing and revising essays, developing interview skills, making connections with admissions officers, and filling out financial aid forms.

High school counselors are dealing with thousands of kids and have little time to get to know students on a personal level. Trevor has always worked one on one with me and made himself available when I need help.

He is dedicated to making every one of his clients stand out amongst the thousands of college applications being submitted. Trevor is so devoted to making sure all his clients feel like they are the only one he is working with. My mother was overjoyed when she saw that I got accepted to six private colleges & universities with award packages that averaged $27,897 per year!"

You Are In for A Big Financial Surprise!

These comments from my former students are precious. This is a young man who did not have the best grades and test scores. In fact, his grades and scores were

17

average. Despite this, he was accepted to six private colleges and universities with an average financial aid offer of $27,897 per year because he followed my advice. As a result, he got into his dream school and received enough free money to make paying for college painless and easily affordable. This, by the way, is my goal for every parent and every student reading this book.

I share these stories with you to help you understand what you can really do with this information, and also to show you that you're learning from someone who doesn't just talk the talk, but walks the walk every day working with families just like yours to get the cost of a four-year degree down to pennies on the dollar.

The truth is, if you have kids and you want them to go to college, without this information the chances are that you are in for a big financial surprise. The cost for going to a local state or city college is now between $18,000 to $35,000 per year; the big time, high-name recognition universities like Harvard, Yale, Cornell, Dartmouth, Boston University, Johns Hopkins, etc., cost between $40,000 and $70,000 ... PER YEAR!

With today's sagging economy, many families have simply been unable to pay that kind of money to send their kids to school. As a result, they use their retirement money and savings. They mortgage their homes to cover the costs of college tuition, travel expenses, room, and board. Or, they do what they can and tell their kids they need to take out student loans, or simply go to an overcrowded community college where most students are taking 3-4 years to get an Associate's degree.

Don't let this potential financial disaster happen to you. And don't disappoint your kids by saying that you simply can't afford to pay for their college education. Now is the time to be smart and show them how to get what they want without paying "full-boat" retail for college. Show them how to pay wholesale for a first-class education with the tools in this book.

By now you are probably asking yourself, "What's the secret? How can I show them how to do this when I don't know how to do it myself?" That's a good question with an easy answer. The way to show them how to do this is for you and your child to read every page of this book and discuss the most important topics as a family.

In this book, you'll learn how to tell if there is (and approximately how much) scholarship and grant money you can qualify for, how to do a preliminary calculation just like the colleges and universities do to compute what you're expected to pay per year for college, and what your child can do to get a five to six figure financial award package.

This Is The Key to Getting Scholarships, Grants & Financial Aid:

This is really the key to getting financial aid. Most people don't know this, but you will. You see, when you fill out your FAFSA and CSS Profile (financial aid forms), the financial aid offices enter your data into an equation that is actually a sophisticated algorithm.

This algorithm is used to calculate the exact amount of money your family is expected to contribute to your child's education.

If you don't fill out this form properly, the chances of you qualifying for substantial financial aid are very low.

If you make a mistake and don't fill it out properly, you can later submit an appeal for more financial aid, but it is always easier to get money the first time around rather than going back and changing your financial aid application information.

There are also many great colleges and universities that award money based on your grades, test scores and unique attributes, such as your extracurricular activities, demonstrated leadership, special talents, and unique experiences. For these top schools, even having slightly above grades, SAT/ACT scores and other merits qualifies you to receive huge chunks of money. I will list many of these schools in this book—and believe me, they are among the top schools in America.

Many parents think they earn too much to get free money for college. What most don't realize is that parents with incomes of $400,000 per year to $600,000 per year are getting scholarships and grants, saving tens of thousands of dollars per year and sending their children to the best universities in America. Meanwhile many parents earning less than $25,000 per year do not know how to qualify for financial aid to pay for college. I am on a mission to show parents of high school students how they can do it too!

It's amazing how few parents and students understand the "truth" about college financial aid and how to make the dream of giving their children a college education a reality.

The truth is, with a little advanced planning and a couple of good strategies, you can get most (if not all) the money you need to pay for your children to go to the best colleges in America for very little out-of-pocket cash and no second mortgages —and, you can minimize student loans.

A Win/Win Strategy For Parents Who Have The Money For College

Of course, some families are well prepared for the cost of college. But even these well-to-do families find value in guiding their children through the process of getting financial aid to pay for college. In fact, some families engineer a program where they match every dollar of scholarship money they get to help pay for school in the form of a graduation bonus. This gives their student the incentive to get all the free money they can so that they graduate with a five or six figure bankroll to pay for graduate school, start their own business, buy their own car, home, pay for their wedding, etc. It also gives the student a sense of *"ownership"* in his or her education.

It's proven to be a good strategy for the parents and students. It gives everyone options of what to do with the money rather than throwing it down the "college tuition rat-hole." It gives the student an opportunity to earn large sums of cash at graduation for lowering their family's out-of-pocket cash to pay for college.

It's About More Than Just Money!

But you'll accomplish more than finding the money for college. You'll find out which colleges fit your child's interests best and which ones have the most generous offers. I'll also show your student step-by step how to get accepted to the colleges of their dreams; the colleges that have the courses and curriculum that will allow them to graduate with a marketable degree that will make it possible for them to get a good job upon graduation.

Here's A Quick List Of The Topics We'll Cover:

- How to avoid going into massive debt or using up all your family's retirement savings to pay for your degree?
- **What you can do to get free scholarships and even if you're a middle income family that is "ineligible" for financial aid.**
- How to get your child admitted to the most selective and prestigious US colleges?

21

- **How to get your child into the top 500 US colleges and universities even if their GPA is below a 3.0?**
- Secrets to motivate your student to prepare for college and future success, even if they have no idea what they want to do with their life.
- **Guidance on what kind of college will be perfect for your student.**
- How to win the largest and least competitive scholarships?
- **How to spot and avoid the many expensive and dangerous scholarship scams that prey on students and parents?**
- What to do if you have been denied financial aid?
- **What to do if you don't feel like you got a fair financial aid offer?**
- Which loans do you avoid like the plague? These so-called "student loan" traps that could cost you $50,000 or more in unnecessary interest and fees—all of which is paid directly to the government and banks!
- **The top FAFSA and CSS Profile mistakes to avoid when filling out financial aid forms. These mistakes could cost you tens of thousands of dollars in free aid.**
- The secrets to get the most scholarships and financial aid for your student if you are recently divorced or are a struggling, single parent.
- **Why saving for college can be dangerous if done the wrong way. There are strategic ways to save for college without disqualifying your student from financial aid in the process.**
- Proven strategies for applying, saving, and paying for college if your income fluctuates.

22

- **How to help your student if he or she wants to major in a field that is very unique?**
- And much more…

How Valuable Is This Information?

It's incredibly valuable. In fact, the information, strategies and techniques I reveal helped me get FREE grants and aid so I could graduate Boston University with a 4-year degree in Business Administration specializing in accounting… and I had a 2.8 GPA when I was in high school applying to colleges!

The Amazing College Secrets Of A Genius Who Got $178,000 To Attend A Top American University!

I am often asked what my secret to success is when it comes to getting kids into great colleges with huge award packages to pay for tuition, books, room, and board.

My success came from my own personal need. Ironically, I come from a family of teachers and when it came time for me to think about going to college, my grades were so average, community college was my only option.

But I wanted to go to a top, private college (Boston University) that cost over $50,000 per year. I love my parents no matter what, yet I couldn't see how they could pay $50,000 per year without borrowing the money. Plus I knew my younger brother would also need their help paying for college.

With a GPA of 2.8, I quit the football team and spent hours at libraries, coffee shops and bookstores, focusing on my grades and SAT scores. I also became an expert at what colleges would give me free money and what colleges would ask me to take on student loans.

What I Learned Paid Off For Me & It Can Do The Same for You!

I became obsessed with college admissions and how to get scholarships and grants. My goal was to get into Boston University, and to get it paid for so I wouldn't graduate with almost $200,000 in student loans. What I learned was amazing and it paid off — big time!

I got a full 4-year financial award valued at $178,000. It didn't cover all the costs, but I was able to graduate with a degree in accounting owing just over $35,000 for all four years.

I was so good at getting free money scholarships and grants that when I graduated, my first job offer was to work for a financial planning company.

They immediately put me to work as a college planner helping their clients' kids get into the colleges of their choosing, and getting the money to pay for tuition and many of their other expenses.

I became so focused and successful at finding the money to pay for a kid's college education, I created a company that specializes in getting kids into their top choice colleges and finding the money to pay for it. That company is appropriately called *College Funding Remedies*.

Since 2009, I've used this information to help more than 200 students grab over $12 million dollars in FREE grants and aid that NEVER has to be paid back.

Why Did I Write This Book For Families & Students?

After my own success in learning how to get a 4-year degree for pennies on the dollar, I devoted my life and career to helping parents and students learn the truth about paying for college and what it takes to get accepted to the college of your choice. But then I realized that there are more families who need my help than I could ever work with personally.

So I wrote this book because I don't want your student to major in debt for the first 10 or 15 years after they graduate. I want your child to graduate with career opportunities and connections, so they can become a consummate professional and financially independent adult.

Why Reading This Book Can't Wait!

It's simple. The longer you wait, the harder it is to get the maximum dollars and help your child get into their "dream" school. College is competitive and getting "all your ducks in a row" takes time—so START NOW to maximize results.

Many parents think, *"Hey, my child is a freshman or a sophomore, I've got 2-3 years before I have to deal with college."* Nothing could be further from the truth. Just recently the government made changes that require colleges to ask about the income parents and students earned two years prior to attending college. This means that colleges will be looking at what you earned in your kid's sophomore and junior year to determine how much you have to pay.

If your kid's a freshman, believe me, this will be the fastest 3 years of your life. It will be a time warp where you wake up one day and your toothless toddler is now a teen getting ready to go to college.

As a parent of a freshman, you've already had 14 years to prepare for this moment. Many parents I meet never thought for a minute they wouldn't have enough money to send their children to college. They say they thought they'd have more time, but along the way something happened. A job was lost, somebody died or got sick, a bad investment or business partnership robbed them of the money they earned and saved. Then long behold the day comes when they have just a few months to come up with the money they thought they'd have by now.

Until now you've always been able to come through for your son or daughter– you've always been able to pull a rabbit out of a hat – even at the last minute. But this time it's different because this time the rabbit has an $80,000-$280,000 price tag on it and a quarter of this money is due every year ($20,000-$70,000 PER YEAR!)

And believe me, those rabbits are a nightmare to pull out of the hat, especially at the last minute. In fact they're pretty much impossible – because it means you're going to have to make a $2,000 to $7,000 (per month) tuition payments, or sign endless trails of student loan applications for the next 4 years. And if you have more than one child, just imagine doubling or tripling those numbers!

If you hesitate and don't take action now, this process will steamroll right over you and suddenly you'll be scrambling to figure out how to come up with the cold, hard cash just to send your kids to a good school, or you'll have to tell your kids that you don't have the money and they should just go to a community college where most of the students don't end up graduating with a 4-year degree, and those who do take 7 years to finish.

Please don't wait until this is your only alternative. In this book, I will give you tips you can use immediately to get the money you need to pay for college. I'm not talking about student loans and borrowing money from your bank or taking out a second mortgage on your home or rental properties.

I'm talking about grants, easy-to-get scholarships, and financial aid packages that help cover the enormous cost of tuition, student fees, room and board. This is money you don't have to pay back.

A Recent Note From Grateful Parents...

"Trevor, We just wanted to contact you to say thanks. Our daughter has decided to go to Tulane University. It was your suggestion that got her interested in the school, so we are very appreciative of your input. The advice and feedback you provided to her in the admissions process was very helpful. She received merit scholarships for $68,000, plus another $22,000 in financial aid (total amount over 4 years is $90,000). Again, thanks for your valuable help. Best wishes."

--Ken & Sandra from San Dimas, CA

Can This Book Really Help You?

The materials, resources and strategies in this book have helped families across the entire spectrum of circumstances, from blue collar families to wealthy families who believe they must bear the entire cost of education. This book is specifically written for families that earn $60,000 - $500,000 per year, although it has also helped families at every income level receive grants, scholarships and aid. These families include:

- **Parents who want their child to attend a prestigious college or university without taking student loans**
- Parents who want their child to have a traditional college experience such as living in on-campus apartments or dorms, instead of commuting to college and living at home
- **Parents who want to avoid sending their child to a community college**
- Families whose college savings accounts do not exceed $200,000 per child
- **Parents who will have more than one child attending college at the same time, especially twins or triplets**

27

- Parents who send their children to a public or charter high school, and therefore do not have a tuition bill factored into their monthly budget
- **Families who want to avoid making tuition or educational loan payments over $3,500 per month or $8,750 per quarter when sending their child to a 4-year college or university**
- Parents who want to avoid using their retirement funds or pensions to pay for college
- **Divorced or separated parents who have not agreed or discussed which parent will pay for college and how much**
- Single parents who will pay for college on their own, especially those who do not receive spousal or child support
- **Parents who are equally (or more) concerned with paying college, than getting their child accepted to college**
- Parents with children who receive financial assistance to attend a private, college preparatory high school
- **Parents of college-bound athletes, who will not play Division 1 sports**
- Small business owners who want to avoid using business assets or equity to pay for college
- **Real estate owners who want to avoid selling or borrowing from their properties to pay for college**
- Parents of homeschooled, college-bound children
- **Parents uncertain about their income stability when their children attend college**
- Retired parents who want to avoid going back to work to pay for college
- **Parents who are not sure what they can comfortably afford to spend per year on college**

When Is The Best Time To Get Free Money Scholarships & Grants To Pay For College?

As the expert on paying for college, parents often ask me when is the best time to get free money in the form of scholarships and grants. The answer is simple, but how you get to the answer is not.

The best time to get the free money you are seeking to help pay for your student's college education is now October of their senior year. That's the time when the colleges and universities are flush with scholarship and grant money.

When the "free money" gets low, or is gone, it naturally becomes increasingly difficult to get any free money.

The Most Expensive Way In The World To Pay For College!

In fact, if you wait too long, the only way to get money for college is through student loans and parent loans. This is an easy (but unbelievably expensive) way to pay for college. Why? It's expensive because you (or your child), could easily pay an additional $50,000 to $125,000+ in interest and finance charges.

The not so simple answer to this question often shocks parents: your best chance of getting the big money actually starts between the 7th and 10th grades. Some parents gasp when I tell them this. That's because they think that the 12th grade is the appropriate time to start planning for college.

In the old days this was probably true. However, today everything has changed. The government and colleges has revised the deadlines to earlier dates to

29

expedite the financial aid process. And college cost much more than ever before. In fact, the only thing more expensive in life than a college degree right now is the purchase of a family home in a nice neighborhood, or paying for a catastrophic illness if you have no health insurance.

If you are the parent of a college-bound high school student, today is your lucky day. Today is the day you find out how to pay for college wholesale and save yourself and your student tens of thousands of dollars. This is where the planning begins so you can maximize your financial aid, encourage your children to go to the school of their dreams, and enjoy the whole college experience without getting a financial heart attack.

Congratulations on finding this book. If you need any clarification on the information presented, or if you just want to take a closer look to see if I am the real deal or get plugged into our community, you can:

- Visit my website at: www.collegefundingremedies.com
- Attend one of my upcoming workshops or webinars at www.collegefundingremedies.com/workshops
- Call my office direct at 1-626-657-7887 and schedule a free one-hour strategy session to see if I can really live up to my promise of saving you tens of thousands of dollars on paying for your child's college education.

In the next chapter, I'm going to reveal to you a very important plan to pay for college that most parents and students don't realize until it's too late.

Part One: Let's Talk About Your Plan To Pay For College

Chapter 1: How Much Money Does College Really Cost?

"The only thing more expensive than education is ignorance."
— Benjamin Franklin

So how much money does college cost these days? In order to answer this question, we first need to agree on what to consider a college cost and non-college cost. The Department of Education uses the term "Cost of Attendance" (COA) to describe the yearly cost to attend college.

Cost of Attendance is one year's cost of tuition,

How Much Money Does College Really Cost?

$268,848 ($67,212/yr.)

From Florida:
$85,760 or ($21,440/yr.)

Not From Florida:
$152,776 or ($38,194/yr.)

From California:
$133,280 or ($33,320/yr.)

UNIVERSITY of WASHINGTON

From Washington:
$108,136 or ($27,034/yr.)

Not From California:
$244,792 or ($56,198/yr.)

Not From Washington:
$192,924 or ($48,231/yr.)

books, room and board, transportation, medical insurance, and fees. Often when parents and students talk about how much a college costs per year, they are only referring to the tuition; however, when planning for college, we need to plan for more than just tuition.

A private school, public school and a community college all have different Costs of Attendance. In fact every school has a slightly different Cost of Attendance.

The Cost of Attendance at a private school is anywhere between $45,000 to $70,000 per year. The cost of a public school is between $18,000 and $35,000 per year if you're considered an in-state resident. If you're not an in-state resident, a state school costs between $32,000 and $55,000 per year.

Lastly, calculating the Cost of Attendance at a community college is quite tricky because often community college students live with their parents. But in order to compare apples to apples we have to calculate what it would cost if a student rented a room, bought their own meals, and had to pay for gas and other transportation on their own. If we include books, tuition, room and board, the average cost to attend a community college is between $8,000 and $16,000 dollars.

You must also keep in mind that the cost of tuition increases by 7-8% per year. This means that right now tuition doubles every 10 years. This also means that if your tuition at a private school is $42,000—just tuition, none of the other costs—the tuition would go up by about $3,150 per year. It is very important when setting up a college budget to keep this inflation rate in mind.

We must also remember that when we mention Cost of Attendance, we are talking about one year's cost. So we must multiply these numbers by at least four (4) in order to get a ballpark of our cost of college for each child. And if we have more than one college-bound child, we need to consider the cost of college for the entire family.

For most families, college can be a very large financial commitment. We must remember however that college has a very high return on investment because the difference between the earnings of someone with a high school diploma versus a 4-year college degree is between $400,000 and $1,000,000 over a lifetime.

The next chapter will explain how most families approach paying for college and you will discover what strategy is the most effective.

Chapter 2: How Are Families Paying For College?

"If a man empties his purse into his head, no one can take it away from him. An investment in knowledge always pays the best interest."
— Benjamin Franklin

It's important to understand how most parents approach paying for college because oftentimes parents keep this a secret or tend to exaggerate what they had to or did not have to do in order to pay for college amongst their peers. It's also important for you to know which decision you are the closest to making so that you plan accurately. You may have a very generous financial aid offer from a college but still have a portion of the college expense that you are expected to pay. It would be unfortunate to get $45,000 per year in scholarship money but then have to put yourself in six figure student loan debt to fund the rest of the money.

Savings Accounts

The first way that families pay for college is by using their college savings accounts. These accounts can be their 529 Plans, UTMA/UGMAs, Educational IRAs, Coverdell ESAs or Savings Bonds.

However, the average amount of money saved in a 529 Plan in 2014 was $20,474. Having seen that a 4-year colleges cost between $18,000 and $70,000 per year, we can see that in most cases, even the people that have 529 Plans have at best a year's worth of college expenses reserved.

If the family does not have any college savings accounts, they often use their life savings to pay for college.

Instead of College Savings, Many Parents Will Spend Their <u>Life Savings</u> on College

Family Life Savings

- **529: $20,474**
- **Retirement: $576,000**
- **911 Savings: $75,000**

College Cost Per Child

W

UNIVERSITY *of*
WASHINGTON

Not From Washington: $192,924 or ($48,231/yr.)

For instance, a family may use their emergency fund or their retirement savings to pay for college. In the example above this family has a 529 Plan and an emergency fund. If the family liquidated their 529 and emergency fund to pay for college, they would still be $97,450 short in the circumstance of sending their child to a college that cost $192,924.

Installment Plans

If a family does not have enough money saved to pay for college, they often make payments to the college. Colleges usually take payments over 3 to 10 installments. This means that if a parent is paying for a $25,000 school, they are making payments of $6,250 per quarter or $2,500 per month.

Many parents do this; however, if they have more than one child, it becomes difficult when more than one kid is going to college at the same time because $2,500 per month can turn into $5,000 per month in college expenses for the family.

Years	Child 1	Child 2	Total Per Month
Year 1	$2,500 Per Month		$2,500 Per Month
Year 2	$2,500 Per Month		$2,500 Per Month
Year 3	$2,500 Per Month	$2,500 Per Month	$5,000 Per Month
Year 4	$2,500 Per Month	$2,500 Per Month	$5,000 Per Month
Year 5	Graduated	$2,500 Per Month	$2,500 Per Month
Year 6	Graduated	$2,500 Per Month	$2,500 Per Month

If the parent does not have the cash flow to pay $2,500 per month, they are offered parent and student loans to pay for college.

Educational Loans

Colleges make it very easy for you to find loans for parents to use to pay for college. The most common loan is the Parent Loan for Undergraduate Students (PLUS Loan). This loan is often picked because it is backed by the federal government, and the loan typically has a lower interest rate than a private student loan. Right now this parent loan has a 6.84% interest rate and a 4.272% origination fee. You can only take out a parent loan once per year for the amount that you owe on college costs and each loan is paid for over a period of 10 years.

Below is a schedule of payments that a parent has to make on parent loans on a school that costs a little over $48,000 per year.

Year in College	Loan Amount	Monthly Payment
Freshman Yr.	$50,383.40	$580.84
Sophomore Yr.	$100,766.80	$1,161.68
Junior Yr.	$151,150.20	$1,742.52
Senior Yr.	$201,533.60	$2,323.36

These payments remain at $2,323.36 per month until 5 years after the student has graduated or when the parent has finally paid off the loan taken out for the freshman year. And if the family pays the loan over a 10 year period, by the time the family has paid the loan back, they have paid $278,803.20. $77,272 of the cost is just interest. (This adds another two years of college expenses in the form of interest.) Many parents ask why the parents often take on the loans instead of the students. The reason for this is that most student loans have higher interest rates at approximately 6.24-11.49% and they often require a cosigner anyway.

Scholarships

Scholarships can be divided into two major categories: private scholarships and college endowment scholarships. Examples of private scholarships are the Nelson Mandela Scholarship, American Rhodes Scholarship, The Holocaust Scholarship or the Gates Millennium Scholarship.

Private scholarships are not the best places to start when looking for free money for college. If you consider all the sources, you'll notice most of the money comes from the federal and state governments and the colleges. In fact, only 5-7% of all free money given out to college-bound students come from private scholarships.

The federal government disburses approximately $170 billion in federal student aid for higher education per year. Colleges also typically award between $14 and $23 billion dollars each year to students from their own endowment funds, and the State of California awards another one billion dollars in California Grants each year to California residents attending schools in California. Conversely, Fasteweb.com, which is the top source for online scholarships, advertises only 3.3 billion dollars in scholarships on their site. So many families fight over the 5-7% of the pie when there are so many colleges that will gladly give them the money they need to pay for college. Furthermore, many of the private scholarships are not four year awards and seldom cover the Cost of Attendance at any college.

If you're applying for private scholarships because you think the federal government, colleges, and your state categorizes you as high income, I still suggest you read the next few chapters very carefully and apply the advice. Even if your family is very affluent, there are still better ways to use your time to get more money for college. What is the alternative? Instead of budgeting all this time in search of online private scholarships to apply for, budget some of that time for the search of schools that are generous with financial aid and merit scholarships.

Going To The
Least Expensive College

The least expensive schools tend to give out the least scholarships and take the longest to graduate their students. What you'll find is that because of the amount of students in the class, there often aren't enough chairs for all the students if the entire class all showed up at the same time. So if there's a mid-term and you show up late for the exam, you end up sitting on the floor. Or if your student wants to attend office hours for a professor or teacher's assistant, all the students that need help cannot fit in the instructor's office for additional guidance.

There also often not enough classes for every student who wants to study a particular major or take a particular class, so several colleges will consider certain majors at their university as "impacted" which means they can no longer accepts students who want to study a popular major. Or the student has to earn an incredibly high college grade point average (3.8 GPA) in order to declare a major that the college is famous for.

Finally at many state colleges when registering for classes, they often fill up within 15 minutes. It is also very common that students need to take classes during the summer to graduate on time. (This costs more money, and more importantly takes more time.)

Most community colleges in the United States have an average graduation rate of 3 years with many colleges having less than 20% graduate in less than 3 years or transferring to 4-year college.

At many state schools, the case is the same. In 2008, 12% of Cal Poly Pomona students graduated in 4 years and 50% graduate in 6 years.

At a school where most students graduate in 6 years, during the 5th and 6th year at the college, the student is still in school accumulating more debt and spending more money on tuition when they should already be earning income from full-time work. We have to add the salary the student should have been earning in order to compare to the cost of attending a 6 year college to the cost of a slightly more expensive 4 year college. We will discuss this in more detail when talk about graduation rates in chapter 5.

Chapter 3: What Most Parents Will Never Know About Getting Scholarships and Grants

"The highest form of ignorance is when you reject something you don't know anything about."
— Wayne Dyer

Now let me show you some of the myths in this process and then we'll start talking about the tools you can use once you understand how things really work.

"My Income Is Too High To Get Grant Money"

Many parents think that their income is too high to get scholarships and grants. What most don't know is that income is one factor among several that colleges use to determine how much money to offer to a parent. The reason this usually happens is that the family does not understand who would give scholarships, grants and financial aid to a family of their category type or how they should present themselves to a college. The other reason is that many parents don't complete financial aid forms at all or when they do, they make mistakes that will disqualify them from getting any money.

"My Kid's Grades Are Too Low To Get A Scholarship"

As you know, I had a 2.8 GPA when my senior year came around to apply to colleges. Your financial aid award, for the exception of merit-based aid, has little to do with your grades.

Once you're admitted to a school, the financial aid office applies a formula that allows them to see if there is any money they can give you. Many colleges don't look at your grades when they are deciding on your aid package. They are looking at whether you "need" the money or not.

I've also worked with many students with GPAs below a 3.0 who have gotten well over $25,000 per year in scholarships, grants and financial aid. A student's talent can also be a basis for getting scholarships. For instance if a student is applying to an art or music school, the student's audition or portfolio has more to do with their chances of getting scholarships than their grades.

"I Live In A Nice Area And My House Is Worth Over A Million Bucks"

Parents with homes worth well over $3 million can qualify for financial aid because there are many colleges that do not ask for their home equity or home value. Despite this, many parents will list this number under their net worth on their financial aid forms. If a school asks you to complete a FAFSA (Free Application for Federal Student Aid) and no other financial aid form, they will not know of or care about your home value or home equity. There are colleges that use forms that will ask for your home equity; however, if they use the FAFSA only, they will not.

If you have over $150,000 in home equity, it is important to know which schools will ask your home equity and which ones will not. Most colleges do not ask for home equity. In fact, there are only about 300 colleges that ask about home equity when they determine if you qualify for financial aid.

In chapter 5, I will list several colleges that do not ask for your home equity based on which financial aid forms they use.

"Only Minorities Get Scholarships"

Financial aid is seldom based on a special group qualification like minority status; it is based primarily on financial need, academic merits or talent. This means that if you are *not* a minority, but have a "financial need," strong academic merit, or talent, you will qualify for aid, so long as you are applying to a school that has free money to give out.

This also means that if you *are* a minority, you must realize that your minority status is not the major component that will be your ticket to getting free money for college. If you have strong academic merit, and you are also a minority, there are colleges that will receive this well; however, they must be interested in giving money to this category of family and have the money to give out.

"All You Have To Do To Get Free Money For College Is Fill Out A FAFSA"

You must complete a financial aid form to present yourself with every opportunity to get financial aid. However, to be certain that you get the money you need, your family must apply to colleges that have the money to give out. (This is where the effort must be applied.)

You must be admitted to colleges that are willing to pay for you to attend. Many parents think that all there is to getting free money is to fill out a financial aid form, but you must plan ahead to know what the best colleges are for your financial situation. If the school doesn't have any money, it doesn't matter if you qualify for funds. You could be considered financially destitute and not receive a single grant from simply filling out a FAFSA, if the schools you're applying to have no (or not enough) money to offer you.

To be clear, if you wait until when it's time to fill out your financial aid forms to start planning for financial aid, you will have too many critical things to do in a very short period of time. And if it turns out that your plan is too idealistic, you will not have enough time to change it before all the good colleges close off their application periods for admission. Planning for scholarships and grants is about knowing how much money a college will give you before you apply as well as knowing what your chances are of getting into a college that has the money to offer you.

Chapter 4: How to Maximize Scholarships & Grants So You Get A Ton Of Money

"I am thankful to all those who said no. It's because of them I did it myself."
— Albert Einstein

For the parent of a college or college-bound student, the most important acronym you must know if you're trying to get scholarships and grants is EFC. EFC stands for Expected Family Contribution. Your Expected Family Contribution (EFC) is the minimum your family will be expected to pay out-of-pocket for each year of college.

It's all about your EFC, EFC, EFC. It's what the government and the colleges expect you to pay for college per year. The lower your EFC, the more need-based financial aid you can get. To get an estimate of your EFC, simply Google "EFC Calculator," and you can quickly calculate what you're expected to contribute to your child's annual college tuition. It's your responsibility to know what your EFC is because it is the most important calculation you need to make to receive maximum need-based financial aid.

The calculation for your EFC is based on the information you submit on your Free Application for Federal Student Aid (FAFSA) and CSS Profile. Although many questions on the FAFSA and CSS Profile will ultimately determine your EFC, here is a list of the top 6 factors that affect it:

1. Parent's Income
2. Parent's Assets
3. Student's Income
4. Student's Assets

5. Total number of members in household
6. Number of kids currently enrolled in college

Before you fill out any financial aid forms, get an accurate estimation of your EFC, so you have an idea of what you have to pay and what questions they will ask you. You may also have an opportunity to minimize your EFC before sending our financials to your student's colleges.

The financial aid process has been newly designed so that all your financial aid forms are due by October of your kid's senior year. This is the month when you find out your EFC. This is also the time when your child is applying to colleges. Then as early as November and as late as April, you will find out how much financial aid you received and how you much you have to pay. Then in August right before your kid starts college, the payment is due.

The big question is: "When would you want to know how much you're expected to pay for college?" Would you want to know how much you're going to pay and receive in grants and scholarships before your child applies to a college, during or after? With proper planning you can know how much money you will receive in aid. This can prevent you and your child from selecting colleges that don't have an intention to give you grants or scholarships.

To have an advantage you must go to a search engine and search for "EFC calculator." The EFC calculator will ask you a couple of questions and give you a ballpark figure of what you're expected to pay when you complete a FAFSA and a CSS Profile. Remember that your Expected Family Contribution can change. It's just a starting point and there are steps you can take to arrive at your lowest EFC. It's like tax planning. Sometimes your answers to only two or three questions or line items can make all the difference in what you have to pay.

For example, a child's assets count heavily towards your EFC. Every dollar a child has in assets—that includes bank accounts or trust funds—accounts for about 20 cents on the dollar. Also every dollar a child makes in income above $6,130 (the limit for 2015-16 aid) cuts their possible award by 50 cents.

Two years before you complete your forms, you can consider spending the child accounts first. You can also transfer the child's accounts into parent accounts because the parents' assets are calculated at a lower rate. If you have $10,000 in a child's saving account, colleges will ask for approximately $2,000 towards the cost of a college; however, if the money is under a parents' name, the colleges will ask for $800. When you make these kinds of changes, be aware of the tax implications as well. For instance, let's say you and your child liquidate a $40,000 UTMA. If this sale causes you to realize a $27,000 capital gain, your child will have to file taxes and include $27,000 worth of income on their financial aid forms. Since the student's income counts more heavily toward your EFC, than a student asset, you may have done yourself more harm than good making this transaction. Finally, some assets will require that the funds are used appropriately for the benefit of the child. Always ask your financial advisor what your capital gain would be if you were to liquidate an asset before doing so, as it may singlehandedly eliminate your eligibility for grants.

Here's an example showing how much an EFC can decrease with planning and an accurate understanding how the formulas work:

When we met Jeremy's parents, they showed me how much they had in college savings accounts and told me that because of the market, their accounts had not earned anything above what they funded with contributions. Jeremy wanted to work for NASA. With his 4.3 weighted

GPA from a public high school and a SAT Score of 2150, he was looking at some of the most competitive schools for his field such as Princeton, Yale, and Johns Hopkins. Most of the schools under consideration accepted less than 13 percent of applicants.

We reviewed the family's Expected Family Contribution (EFC). Based on the calculated number, it computed that this family could afford up to $99,999 in college expenses in any given year! That was ridiculous; their income was $60,493 for the previous year.

After reviewing the clients' assets, we identified that this was where the problem lay. The assets this family had saved were for the purposes of retirement, but the EFC calculator factored those assets into their ability to pay for college. Because of how the questions were worded in the two financial aid forms, the family did not know which assets they needed to include on the forms, and which assets were not necessary to mention.

By making these adjustments, repositioning the family's assets, and finding the most reasonable and realistic valuation on their home, we were able to reduce this family's EFC from $99,999 to $8,500 at schools that only take a FAFSA, and $13,420 at schools that require a CSS Profile. (A CSS Profile is a more advanced financial aid form that the most expensive private schools use before they distribute scholarships from their own endowment funds.)

By April, Jeremy was accepted into Johns Hopkins University with an offer of $49,900 in financial aid for the first year alone. He also received offers of $26,920 in financial aid from UC San Diego and a few others. Jeremy decided to go to Johns Hopkins University, and when his father saw me post his son's award letter in my office, he paused for a second, took a deep breath and said "Thank you." He said he not only appreciated the results I created for his family, but the mentorship and motivation that I gave to his son.

Here's another example of a business and real estate owner:

Michael was accepted to DePaul University, but decided not to attend the school. He and his mother decided that Michael would go to Pasadena City College, but he quickly discovered that it would not be easy to get all the classes that he would need in order to transfer in two years. As Michael had been going to a private school, the parents had a budget for college expenses. They also had another son, Sean, in private school at a cost of a little under $18,000 per year. The family owed $29,700 outside of their mortgage. On the parents' personal tax return they declared a property owned by their business. Declaring the property in this way almost entirely disqualified them from receiving financial aid.

We advised Michael to apply to a private junior college that would enable him to complete the necessary classes on time. We explained to Michael's mother that she needed to provide accurate documentation to clarify that the property they owned was a business asset, not a personal asset. Since the business was small, with fewer than 100 employees, it did not have to be listed on the financial aid forms.

After submitting the corrected forms to the junior college, Michael was accepted with an offer of $35,000 in financial aid for his first year.

Here's a brief example of a divorced parent:

With one parent single and another parent remarried, I looked into who had real custody to set the direction of the case. The single father made about $70,000 per year. And his remarried ex-wife's household income was $400,000 per year. The rule is "whoever lives with the student 51% of the time is the custodial parent." So we were able to just use the father's information on the forms when colleges asked. Because of this, the gentleman and his child received about $14,000 per year in scholarships, grants and financial aid.

There are different strategies for different families. I can go on and on. I just want to give you a couple of examples so you understand how this works out in the real world.

It's your responsibility to know what your EFC is and that you know what's available to make sure you're not making mistakes. You should know what strategies are available. It's kind of like the tax world. You're not obligated to pay any more than you're supposed to, so that's essentially how EFC planning works.

Now that you understand your Expected Family Contribution, it's time for us to make estimates of the scholarship and grant money you can expect from colleges.

Chapter 5: The Secret Formula Almost No One Knows

"You have to learn the rules of the game. And then you have to play better than anyone else."
— Albert Einstein

The following equation is the foundation behind how the federal government, state and all U.S. colleges determine a family's eligibility for need-based financial aid:

**Cost of Attendance
(minus) Expected Family Contribution
= Financial Need**

COA – EFC = Need

In other words, total what the school costs and subtract what you're expected to pay. The results will equal your Need (or your eligibility for financial aid).

If we want to increase your need or your eligibility for financial aid, there are three ways to do so with this formula: increase the Cost of Attendance (COA), lower your Expected Family Contribution (EFC), or both!

However, instead of choosing a school with a high Cost of Attendance, parents choose the least expensive school (schools with a low Cost of Attendance). And instead of yielding their lowest Expected Family Contribution, they fill out the financial aid forms at the last minute, make costly mistakes and show the highest Contribution.

If the EFC is high and the COA is low, we eliminate eligibility for aid. But if the EFC is low and the COA is high, we have a substantial "financial need" and as long as we are applying to a college that can give us the money we need, we will get a substantial financial aid offer.

There are two ways that a school will meet your financial Need. A college can give you Gift Aid to meet your financial Need or give you Self-Help. Gift Aid is free money grants and scholarships. Self-help includes work-study and federal student loans. Some of the federal loans can be attractive. For instance, the Stafford loan is an interest-free loan while the student is in college and if the student goes into a particular field like government service or teaching, the loan can be reassessed or forgiven in some cases.

Three Questions To Ask Every School

There are three main questions you must ask every school to determine your net cost to pay for college. First question: what percentage of Need do you meet? Let's say a college's Cost of Attendance is $65,000 and your Expected Family Contribution is $10,000. This means your financial Need is $55,000. This does not mean you will get the $55,000 from the college. They may not meet 100% of your Need.

There are colleges that meet 100% of your Need, and there are also colleges that meet 0% of your Need and everything in between. You must know what percent of "Need" a college meets. And if you need the most scholarships and grants possible, you must first apply to colleges that meet 70% to 100% of need (more on this in a few more pages).

If you have a low EFC but you are going to a school that gives a low percent of Need, this means that even though you need the money, you will not be given any because the school does not give out enough money to families that need it. This is not because of your income. It is because the college doesn't have the money.

54

The next question to ask a college is: what percent of the money that you give me will be gift-aid versus self-help? When a school offers you money, a portion of that money will be grants and scholarships and another portion will be work study and student loans. Most colleges don't offer 100% free money. Some of the money they offer will be work-study and some federal student loans like the Federal Direct Subsidized Loan. The ratio of free money to work-study and federal loans could be 80/20, 60/40, or it could be 50/50. This depends on the school's policy.

The last question is: how long does it take to graduate from your school? As mentioned before, if your student is attending a $20,000 per year college where most students take 6 years to graduate, the total cost is $120,000 for the education ($20,000 times 6 years), instead of $80,000 ($20,000 tuition, books, etc. times 4 years). In fact, sending your child to a $20,000 per year school with a 6-year graduation rate can cost the same as sending them to a $30,000 per year school with 4-year graduation rate. Moreover, when you factor in the salary the student would have made had he or she graduated on time, the total cost becomes higher.

For instance, if the student could command $35,000 per year salary with a degree their first two years out of college, but instead spend an additional $20,000 per year trying to finish the 5th and 6th year of school, the true cost of the $20,000 per year with a 6-year graduation rate is $190,000.

How Much Does It Really Cost To Attend A School With A 6-Year Graduation Rate?

($20,000 tuition, books, etc. X 6 years) + ($35,000 lost income X 2 years) = $190,000

Although sending your child to an inexpensive college might appear the most economical, if this child does not graduate on time, this college can in fact become your most expensive option.

Now It's Time To Bring This All Together For You

Case Studies:

School A (Pepperdine Univ):
Cost- $40,000
EFC - $10,000
Need - $30,000

School B (Cal Poly Pomona):
Cost- $20,000
EFC - $10,000
Need - $10,000

School A:
Meets 100% need.
Gift aid – 80%
Self help – 20%

School B:
Meets 60% need = $6,000 ($4,000 short!)
Gift aid – 50%
Self help – 50%

What you actually pay at each school:

School A:
Total EFC = **$10,000**
Total Gift = $24,000
Total Self = $6,000

School B:
EFC = $10,000
+ Unmet Need = $4,000
Total EFC = **$14,000**
Total Gift = $3,000
Total Self = $3,000

First, please note that these college cost numbers are simply nice easy estimates for simple math. For instance, Pepperdine does not cost $40,000 per year anymore. It cost $67,152, but I used $40,000 per year to make the math easier. These are just examples to follow.

56

Please follow me on the above diagram. School A is Pepperdine University. And School B is Cal Poly Pomona.

In this example, Pepperdine costs $40,000 (this is the Cost of Attendance). The family pays $10,000 (their Expected Family Contribution or EFC). So this family is eligible for $30,000 in financial aid at Pepperdine.

In this example, Pepperdine meets 100% of their Need, so the family will receive 100% of the $30,000. 80% of the $30,000 Pepperdine offers will be gift-aid (free money), and 20% is self-help (work-study and federal loans).

Of the $30,000 this family receives from Pepperdine, $24,000 will be free money and $6,000 will be self-help (work-study and federal loans).

So in this example, how much does it cost for the family to go to Pepperdine per year? What's the out of pocket?

If you answered $10,000, you are almost correct because the parents are expected to pay $10,000 per year (their Expected Family Contribution). However, the student also has to pay back the $6,000 in self-help they've been offered. So it costs the family a total of $16,000 per year to attend Pepperdine.

Case Studies:

School A (Pepperdine Univ):	School B (Cal Poly Pomona):
Cost- $40,000	Cost- $20,000
EFC- $10,000	EFC - $10,000
Need - $30,000	Need - $10,000
School A:	School B:
Meets 100% need.	Meets 60% need = $6,000 ($4,000 short!)
Gift aid – 80%	Gift aid – 50%
Self help – 20%	Self help – 50%

What you actually pay at each school:

School A:		School B:	
Total EFC =	**$10,000**	EFC =	$10,000
Total Gift =	$24,000	+ Unmet Need =	$4,000
Total Self =	$6,000	Total EFC =	**$14,000**
		Total Gift =	$3,000
		Total Self =	$3,000

Now, let's look at Cal Poly Pomona which costs $20,000 per year in this example. Once again the parent is definitely expected to pay their EFC of $10,000–it is the same at every school that uses the same financial aid forms. Their EFC of $10,000 is also their minimum out of pocket. However, at Cal Poly Pomona (a $20,000 per year school) the parents only have a $10,000 financial Need.

Moreover in this example, Cal Poly Pomona can only meet 60% of this family's financial Need. The family receives only $6,000 from Cal Poly Pomona, because this college can only offer the family 60% of their $10,000 financial Need. In other words, the family needed $10,000, but the school only offered them $6,000, so the family's financial aid offer from Cal Poly Pomona ends up $4,000 short.

Because the college was short $4,000, this amount is added back to the parents' Expected Family Contribution as an Unmet Need. Now, the family's minimum out of pocket for colleges becomes $14,000 ($10,000 in EFC and $4,000 in Unmet Need).

Lastly, although Cal Poly Pomona offered this family $6,000, 50% of the $6,000 offered was actually free money. The other 50% of the offer is work-study and federal loans (self-help).

The family receives $3,000 in free grants from Cal Poly Pomona, and the student receives $3,000 in work study and student loans.

So how much does it cost for this family to attend Cal Poly Pomona in this example? Well, we know that the parent has to pay $14,000. (This is their EFC plus Unmet Need.) The student also has to work to pay off the work study and federal student loans (self-help). So the total cost per year for this family to attend Cal Poly Pomona is $17,000.

In this case study, Pepperdine (the $40,000 school) cost the family $16,000 per year, but Cal Poly Pomona (the $20,000 school) costs the family $17,000. Which cost less? The $40,000 college or the $20,000 college?

The $40,000 per year private college costs this family less than the state college, because they had more free money to offer.

If I may add one more point, not only does the $20,000 per year college cost more money per year in this example, but at this school it takes students longer to graduate. So while this student may graduate from Pepperdine in the traditional four year period at a total cost of $64,000 ($16,000 tuition, books, etc. times 4 years), meanwhile it may take this student up to 6 years to graduate from Cal Poly Pomona. At $17,000 per year times 6 years, that's $102,000! Plus if we add in the lost income from not working full-time those additional two years the student was in college at a salary of $35,000 per year, Cal Poly Pomona would have truly cost this family $174,000. What an amazing difference! One college would cost the family $64,000 total for 4 years. The other, less expensive college would have cost the family $174,000 over 6 years including lost income.

Personally, I'm glad I went to a $50,000 per year university and paid less than $15,000 per year total (between my family and me) to attend. As it turns out, it would have been more expensive if I attended a community college, lived at home and commuted, when you tally up the tuition, books, meals and lost income. I went to a $50,000 per year private school for less than a community college, all because I was accepted to a school that had the money to meet my financial Need. But I'm not the only one! Many parents and students I've shown this to have done the same—and so can you!

Two Main Financial Aid Forms

Free Application For Federal Student Aid (FAFSA)

There are two main financial aid forms: FAFSA and CSS Profile. Both of these forms are the tools used to determine your EFC (the minimum you pay for college). The FAFSA is a 100+ question form due in October. It will ask for the income you've earned two years before your child attends college. Once you file your tax return, it will then ask you to update your FAFSA for what you've earned one year prior to sending your child to college. For instance, if your child graduates in 2017, the college will ask for line items on your 2015 tax return and base your financial award on these numbers initially. Then when you do your 2016 tax return, it will ask you to update the FAFSA with these numbers and show your final offer. If your child graduates college in 2018, the college will ask for your 2016 tax return, and then ask you to update your FAFSA with your 2017 tax return to determine your EFC. When you complete this form, do not include your home equity or retirement qualified retirement accounts. Many parents incorrectly include these assets because the FAFSA does not explicitly ask you to list all your assets; it simply asks you to list your net worth, but if you include your retirement accounts and home equity under your net worth calculation, you could cost yourself a lot of financial aid.

College Scholarship Service Profile (CSS Profile)

The other main financial aid form is the CSS Profile. The CSS Profile is usually an additional form that some private colleges ask you to also complete. The form has a little over 250 questions. Like the FAFSA, the CSS Profile will also ask about income you've earned two years prior to your child attending college, as well as projections of what you will earn the year prior to your child attending college, in order to determine your EFC. In fact, many schools that use a CSS Profile require you to mail or upload your most recent tax returns once you've filed to finalize your EFC. You'll just want to be familiar with this in case your income is vastly different from one year to another.

Finally the CSS Profile does indeed ask about your home equity, qualified retirement accounts, business equity, outside scholarships you've won, non-custodial parent's income, grandparent's commitment to paying for college, etc. It may even ask you the year, make and model of all the cars you own.

If you have a lot of home equity, you must find out whether the colleges your child is applying to will ask you for a CSS Profile. In the chart following, I will show you which colleges ask for a CSS Profile and which do not. The colleges that ask for a CSS Profile will count your home equity, the colleges that use a FAFSA only will not.

If you are completing a CSS Profile, when you list your home market value and amount owed on this form, it will include your home equity as an asset and factor it into your EFC, so be aware of this.

When listing the market value of any asset, it is very important to be conservative in your estimate. List what your home would definitely sell for if you put it upon the market the day you completed the financial aid forms. Be sure to include closing costs and any other expenses to prepare the home or any other asset for final sale. Also, make sure you can substantiate all your estimates if a college ever asks.

Secrets To Getting
The Most Financial Aid
If You're Divorced Or A Single Parent

If you're divorced or a single parent, and your child is applying to colleges that ask for a CSS Profile, many of these colleges will also ask for the non-custodial parent's financial information to determine how much this parent can also afford to contribute. These colleges will ask for the other parent's financial information whether or not they have paid for tuition, child support or alimony in the past.

If your child and your ex-spouse have not communicated in over 2 years, you can complete a Non-custodial Waiver Form to absolve yourself from needing to submit the non-custodial parent's information. Your child will also need to sign this document.

Most colleges that use a CSS Profile ask for the non-custodial parent's information—not all but most. If you're a single or divorced parent and you're concerned about your ex's ability or willingness to pay, you'll want to consider colleges that ask for a FAFSA only or colleges use a CSS Profile, but do not ask for Non-Custodial Profile.

These Colleges Give Out
Gobs Of Free Grant Money

The following chart will give you a list of colleges that offer the most grant money and the average percent of need they meet as well as the SAT (Math and Critical Reading score only) and ACT score it takes the have a great chance of acceptance. Lastly, it also details whether they use a FAFSA, CSS Profile, and a Non-custodial Profile.

Under the column "Form", if the college lists "FAFSA", it means it uses a FAFSA only, and does not use a CSS Profile. If under "Form" it says "CSS", but doesn't say "CSS & NCP", it means the college will ask for a CSS Profile, but will not ask for a Non-Custodial Profile. In other words the colleges that list "FAFSA" or "CSS" will not ask for your ex's finances. The only colleges that will ask for the non-custodial parent's finances will be the ones that say "CSS & NCP." Always check the college's website or give them a call to be sure. Just ask if they require a "Non-Custodial Profile."

Just to reiterate if the college lists "FAFSA" it also will not count your home equity. However if under "Forms" the college lists "CSS" or "CSS & NCP," they will ask for your home equity and include this asset in your Expected Family Contribution.

These Colleges Meet 70% to 100% Of Your Need:

Note: Before you consider any public colleges on this list out of your home state, call the school's financial aid office to make sure they also give adequate financial offers to out-of-state residents. Secondly, this list changes annually, so you must double check your projected offer by running a net price calculator for the school you're considering. Always apply to several colleges. Don't just apply to one college.

College	State	% Need	Form	75% SAT	75% ACT
Alabama State University*	AL	76	FAFSA	960	20
Birmingham-Southern College	AL	75	FAFSA	1240	29
Judson College	AL	83	FAFSA	1220	25
Samford University	AL	70	FAFSA	1240	29
Spring Hill College	AL	90	FAFSA	1200	27
University of Alabama, Huntsville*	AL	71	FAFSA	1320	30
University of Mobile	AL	70	FAFSA	1040	24
Harding University	AR	83	FAFSA	1240	28
Henderson State University*	AR	92	FAFSA	1060	24
Hendrix College	AR	84	FAFSA	1320	31
John Brown University	AR	77	FAFSA	1290	30
Lyon College	AR	82	FAFSA	1130	27
Ouachita Baptist University	AR	84	FAFSA	1170	28
Arizona State University -- Tempe Campus*	AZ	71	FAFSA	1270	28

California Institute of Technology	CA	100	CSS & NCP	1600	35
California State University, Bakersfield*	CA	72	FAFSA	1110	21
California State University, Fresno*	CA	73	FAFSA	1110	21
California State University, Long Beach*	CA	80	FAFSA	1170	25
California State University, San Bernardino*	CA	77	FAFSA	990	20
Chapman University	CA	75	FAFSA	1290	29
Claremont McKenna College	CA	100	CSS & NCP	1520	33
Fresno Pacific University	CA	75	FAFSA	1100	24
Harvey Mudd College	CA	100	CSS & NCP	1570	35
Humboldt State University*	CA	71	FAFSA	1100	24
Marymount California University	CA	89	FAFSA	1010	21
Mills College	CA	86	FAFSA	1250	29
Occidental College	CA	100	CSS & NCP	1390	31
Pepperdine University	CA	77	FAFSA	1330	30
Pitzer College	CA	100	CSS & NCP	1400	31
Pomona College	CA	100	CSS & NCP	1540	34
San Francisco State University*	CA	73	FAFSA	1110	24
San Jose State University*	CA	76	FAFSA	1180	26
Santa Clara University	CA	81	CSS	1390	31
Scripps College	CA	100	CSS & NCP	1460	33
Soka University of America	CA	100	FAFSA	1370	29

St. Mary's College of California	CA	85	FAFSA	1210	27
Stanford University	CA	100	CSS & NCP	1570	34
Thomas Aquinas College	CA	100	CSS & NCP	1350	31
University of California -- Los Angeles*	CA	84	FAFSA	1460	32
University of California at Merced*	CA	88	FAFSA	1130	24
University of California, Berkeley*	CA	89	FAFSA	1490	33
University of California, Davis*	CA	80	FAFSA	1350	31
University of California, Irvine*	CA	84	FAFSA	1340	30
University of California, Riverside*	CA	87	FAFSA	1250	27
University of California, San Diego*	CA	87	FAFSA	1410	32
University of California, Santa Barbara*	CA	83	FAFSA	1380	30
University of California, Santa Cruz*	CA	80	FAFSA	1280	28
University of Redlands	CA	87	FAFSA	1200	27
University of San Diego	CA	73	FAFSA	1320	30
University of Southern California	CA	100	CSS & NCP	1480	33
Westmont College	CA	76	FAFSA	1290	29
Whittier College	CA	80	FAFSA	1170	25
William Jessup University	CA	70	FAFSA	1120	25
Colorado College	CO	100	CSS & NCP	1460	32
Colorado State University*	CO	74	FAFSA	1250	27
Fort Lewis College*	CO	91	FAFSA	1130	24
Regis University	CO	80	FAFSA	1190	27

University of Colorado, Boulder*	CO	81	FAFSA	1290	30
University of Denver	CO	86	CSS & NCP	1300	30
University of Northern Colorado*	CO	78	FAFSA	1160	25
Connecticut College	CT	100	CSS & NCP	1410	31
Fairfield University	CT	87	CSS & NCP	1260	28
Southern Connecticut State University*	CT	70	FAFSA	1030	23
Trinity College	CT	100	CSS & NCP	1340	30
Wesleyan University	CT	100	CSS & NCP	1480	33
Yale University	CT	100	CSS & NCP	1600	35
American University	D.C.	86	CSS & NCP	1340	30
Catholic University of America	D.C.	78	CSS & NCP	1230	28
Gallaudet University	D.C.	73	FAFSA	970	20
Georgetown University	D.C.	100	CSS & NCP	1520	33
The George Washington University	D.C.	89	CSS & NCP	1390	31
Delaware State University*	DE	72	FAFSA	970	20
University of Delaware*	DE	76	FAFSA	1300	29
Eckerd College	FL	88	FAFSA	1240	29
Florida Agricultural & Mechanical University*	FL	73	FAFSA	1030	22
Florida Institute of Technology	FL	83	FAFSA	1270	30
Florida Southern College	FL	74	FAFSA	1220	28
Jacksonville University	FL	86	FAFSA	1110	25
New College of Florida*	FL	91	FAFSA	1380	30

Nova Southeastern University	FL	81	FAFSA	1240	29
Rollins College	FL	77	FAFSA	1280	29
Stetson University	FL	79	FAFSA	1280	28
University of Florida*	FL	99	FAFSA	1360	31
University of Miami	FL	78	CSS & NCP	1420	32
University of North Florida*	FL	91	FAFSA	1230	26
Agnes Scott College	GA	85	FAFSA	1330	29
Armstrong State University*	GA	86	FAFSA	1090	23
Berry College	GA	85	CSS & NCP	1260	29
Brenau University	GA	75	FAFSA	1080	24
Covenant College	GA	84	FAFSA	1280	29
Emmanuel College	GA	72	FAFSA	1130	25
Emory University	GA	100	CSS & NCP	1460	32
Kennesaw State University*	GA	84	FAFSA	1170	24
LaGrange College	GA	75	FAFSA	1130	24
Mercer University	GA	87	FAFSA	1290	29
Middle Georgia State College*	GA	87	FAFSA	n/a	n/a
Oglethorpe University	GA	74	FAFSA	1230	28
Piedmont College	GA	75	FAFSA	1050	23
Point University	GA	85	FAFSA	1190	26
University of Georgia*	GA	81	FAFSA	1350	31
Young Harris College	GA	81	FAFSA	1080	24
Valdosta State University*	GA	100	FAFSA	1100	24
Chaminade University of Honolulu	HI	78	FAFSA	1060	22
Hawaii Pacific University	HI	81	FAFSA	1120	25

University of Hawaii at Manoa*	HI	75	FAFSA	1090	26
Briar Cliff University	IA	88	FAFSA	1090	24
Buena Vista University	IA	100	FAFSA	1160	25
Central College	IA	83	FAFSA	1110	27
Clarke University	IA	76	FAFSA	1120	24
Coe College	IA	87	FAFSA	1280	28
Cornell College	IA	79	FAFSA	1320	29
Dordt College	IA	87	FAFSA	1240	28
Drake University	IA	76	FAFSA	1310	30
Graceland University	IA	76	FAFSA	960	23
Grand View University	IA	85	FAFSA	1040	23
Grinnell College	IA	100	CSS & NCP	1500	33
Iowa State University*	IA	83	FAFSA	1310	29
Loras College	IA	90	FAFSA	1190	25
Luther College	IA	89	FAFSA	1250	28
Morningside College	IA	84	FAFSA	1200	26
Mount Mercy University	IA	77	FAFSA	1160	25
Northwestern College	IA	95	FAFSA	1240	27
Simpson College	IA	89	FAFSA	1240	27
University of Iowa*	IA	71	FAFSA	1320	28
University of Northern Iowa*	IA	76	FAFSA	1160	25
Wartburg College	IA	84	FAFSA	1180	27
Northwest Nazarene University	ID	75	FAFSA	1180	26
The College of Idaho	ID	91	FAFSA	1190	27
University of Idaho*	ID	79	FAFSA	1170	27
Augustana College	IL	84	FAFSA	1260	29
Aurora University	IL	85	FAFSA	1100	24
Bradley University	IL	72	FAFSA	1270	28

Concordia University -- Chicago	IL	74	FAFSA	1130	25
Dominican University	IL	76	FAFSA	1000	24
Elmhurst College	IL	82	FAFSA	1230	26
Eureka College	IL	80	FAFSA	1240	26
Greenville College	IL	76	FAFSA	1100	26
Illinois College	IL	87	FAFSA	1090	26
Illinois Institute of Technology	IL	83	FAFSA	1380	31
Illinois State University*	IL	72	FAFSA	1200	26
Illinois Wesleyan University	IL	88	CSS	1380	30
Knox College	IL	91	FAFSA	1360	30
Lake Forest College	IL	85	FAFSA	1250	28
Lewis University	IL	81	FAFSA	1140	25
Loyola University Chicago	IL	78	FAFSA	1260	29
McKendree University	IL	82	FAFSA	1180	25
Millikin University	IL	88	FAFSA	1190	26
Monmouth College	IL	91	FAFSA	1180	25
North Central College	IL	78	FAFSA	1240	27
Northwestern University	IL	100	CSS & NCP	1560	34
Olivet Nazarene University	IL	86	FAFSA	1240	27
Principia College	IL	99	CSS & NCP	1230	29
Quincy University	IL	81	FAFSA	980	25
St. Xavier University	IL	79	FAFSA	1010	24
Trinity Christian College	IL	74	FAFSA	1180	27
University of Chicago	IL	100	CSS & NCP	1590	35
University of Illinois Springfield*	IL	82	FAFSA	1240	27
University of St. Francis	IL	85	FAFSA	1050	25

Wheaton College	IL	90	CSS	1410	32
DePauw University	IN	89	CSS	1300	29
Earlham College	IN	90	FAFSA	1370	31
Goshen College	IN	82	FAFSA	1260	28
Hanover College	IN	78	FAFSA	1170	28
Huntington University	IN	73	FAFSA	1130	26
Indiana State University*	IN	79	FAFSA	1020	22
Manchester University	IN	70	FAFSA	1110	24
Purdue University -- West Lafayette*	IN	81	FAFSA	1330	30
Rose-Hulman Institute of Technology	IN	76	FAFSA	1420	32
Saint Joseph's College	IN	80	FAFSA	1110	24
Saint Mary's College	IN	85	CSS	1210	28
Taylor University	IN	74	FAFSA	1260	30
Trine University	IN	80	FAFSA	1160	27
University of Evansville	IN	85	FAFSA	1240	29
University of Indianapolis	IN	71	FAFSA	1120	25
University of Notre Dame	IN	100	CSS & NCP	1520	34
University of Saint Francis	IN	73	FAFSA	1060	24
University of Southern Indiana*	IN	77	FAFSA	1100	24
Valparaiso University	IN	89	FAFSA	1220	29
Wabash College	IN	88	CSS	1240	28
Baker University	KS	80	FAFSA	1110	26
Bethel College	KS	87	FAFSA	920	25
Friends University	KS	92	FAFSA	1240	27
Kansas State University*	KS	78	FAFSA	1280	28
McPherson College	KS	94	FAFSA	1110	24
Newman University	KS	79	FAFSA	1090	27
Sterling College	KS	83	FAFSA	1050	24

Asbury University	KY	81	FAFSA	1240	28
Bellarmine University	KY	76	FAFSA	1180	27
Berea College	KY	94	FAFSA	1220	27
Campbellsville University	KY	81	FAFSA	1040	23
Centre College	KY	86	FAFSA	1340	31
Eastern Kentucky University*	KY	85	FAFSA	1120	24
Georgetown College	KY	78	FAFSA	1150	27
Thomas More College	KY	80	FAFSA	1050	23
Transylvania University	KY	87	FAFSA	1300	30
Union College	KY	70	FAFSA	1160	25
University of Pikeville	KY	83	FAFSA	930	23
University of the Cumberlands	KY	79	FAFSA	1080	25
Louisiana State University*	LA	72	FAFSA	1230	27
Loyola University New Orleans	LA	77	FAFSA	1230	28
Tulane University	LA	95	CSS & NCP	1410	32
Amherst College	MA	100	CSS & NCP	1550	34
Assumption College	MA	73	FAFSA	1200	26
Babson College	MA	96	CSS & NCP	1370	30
Bard College at Simon's Rock	MA	78	CSS & NCP	1400	31
Bay Path University	MA	77	FAFSA	1060	23
Bentley University	MA	95	CSS	1330	30
Boston College	MA	100	CSS & NCP	1460	33
Boston University	MA	91	CSS & NCP	1410	31
Brandeis University	MA	95	CSS & NCP	1480	33

Clark University	MA	95	CSS & NCP	1330	31
College of the Holy Cross	MA	100	CSS & NCP	1380	31
Elms College	MA	70	FAFSA	1060	23
Emmanuel College	MA	76	FAFSA	1190	26
Franklin W. Olin College of Engineering	MA	100	FAFSA	1550	34
Gordon College	MA	70	FAFSA	1280	29
Hampshire College	MA	86	CSS & NCP	1350	29
Harvard University	MA	100	CSS & NCP	1600	35
Lasell College	MA	73	FAFSA	1070	23
Massachusetts College of Liberal Arts*	MA	79	FAFSA	1090	23
Massachusetts Institute of Technology	MA	100	CSS & NCP	1570	35
Mount Holyoke College	MA	100	CSS & NCP	1450	31
Northeastern University	MA	100	CSS & NCP	1500	34
Pine Manor College	MA	81	FAFSA	n/a	n/a
Simmons College	MA	76	FAFSA	1260	28
Smith College	MA	100	CSS & NCP	1470	31
Stonehill College	MA	93	CSS & NCP	1220	28
Tufts University	MA	100	CSS & NCP	1520	33
University of Massachusetts Amherst*	MA	80	FAFSA	1310	30
University of Massachusetts Dartmouth*	MA	89	FAFSA	1150	26
University of Massachusetts Lowell*	MA	91	FAFSA	1240	28

University of Massachusetts Boston*	MA	88	FAFSA	1150	26
Wellesley College	MA	100	CSS & NCP	1480	33
Western New England University	MA	73	FAFSA	1170	26
Wheaton College	MA	93	CSS & NCP	1350	28
Williams College	MA	100	CSS & NCP	1560	34
Worcester Polytechnic Institute	MA	79	CSS & NCP	1410	32
Worcester State University*	MA	77	FAFSA	1100	25
Goucher College	MD	79	CSS & NCP	1280	29
Hood College	MD	77	FAFSA	1140	25
Johns Hopkins University	MD	99	CSS & NCP	1530	34
Loyola University Maryland	MD	94	CSS & NCP	1270	29
McDaniel College	MD	90	FAFSA	1200	27
Mount St. Mary's University	MD	76	FAFSA	1150	24
St. John's College	MD	84	FAFSA	1440	32
St. Mary's College of Maryland*	MD	75	FAFSA	1230	28
University of Maryland, College Park*	MD	76	FAFSA	1420	32
Washington College	MD	84	FAFSA	1270	29
Bates College	ME	100	CSS & NCP	1430	32
Bowdoin College	ME	100	CSS & NCP	1520	34
Colby College	ME	100	CSS & NCP	1430	32
College of the Atlantic	ME	96	FAFSA	1340	30

Husson University	ME	73	FAFSA	1050	21
University of Maine*	ME	83	FAFSA	1190	27
University of Maine -- Farmington*	ME	87	FAFSA	1100	26
University of Maine -- Presque Isle*	ME	83	FAFSA	1060	23
University of Maine at Fort Kent*	ME	80	FAFSA	990	19
University of Southern Maine*	ME	76	FAFSA	1110	24
Albion College	MI	86	FAFSA	1210	27
Alma College	MI	72	FAFSA	1320	27
Andrews University	MI	82	FAFSA	1220	27
Aquinas College	MI	78	FAFSA	1200	26
Calvin College	MI	78	FAFSA	1300	29
Central Michigan University*	MI	83	FAFSA	1180	25
Cornerstone University	MI	71	FAFSA	1190	25
Ferris State University*	MI	70	FAFSA	1120	24
Grand Valley State University*	MI	70	FAFSA	1200	26
Hope College	MI	79	FAFSA	1310	29
Kalamazoo College	MI	95	FAFSA	1350	30
Lawrence Technological University	MI	70	FAFSA	1230	28
Michigan Technological University*	MI	79	FAFSA	1350	30
Oakland University*	MI	78	FAFSA	1200	26
Spring Arbor University	MI	82	FAFSA	1160	25
University of Detroit Mercy	MI	71	FAFSA	1310	26
University of Michigan -- Ann Arbor*	MI	85	CSS & NCP	1480	33
Western Michigan University*	MI	75	FAFSA	1160	25

Bethany Lutheran College	MN	84	FAFSA	1200	26
Bethel University	MN	80	FAFSA	1280	28
Carleton College	MN	100	CSS & NCP	1510	33
College of Saint Benedict	MN	92	FAFSA	1250	29
Concordia College -- Moorhead	MN	92	FAFSA	1330	28
Hamline University	MN	85	FAFSA	1180	27
Gustavus Adolphus College	MN	91	FAFSA	1360	30
Macalester College	MN	100	CSS & NCP	1470	32
Martin Luther College	MN	73	FAFSA	1240	27
Minnesota State University -- Mankato*	MN	72	FAFSA	1160	25
Saint John's University	MN	95	FAFSA	1220	28
St. Catherine University	MN	92	CSS & NCP	1230	26
St. Mary's University of Minnesota	MN	90	FAFSA	1160	26
St. Olaf College	MN	99	CSS & NCP	1390	32
The College of St. Scholastica	MN	76	FAFSA	1220	27
University of Minnesota -- Morris*	MN	76	FAFSA	1330	28
University of Minnesota -- Twin Cities*	MN	77	FAFSA	1440	31
University of Minnesota at Crookston*	MN	75	FAFSA	990	24
University of Northwestern -- St. Paul	MN	94	FAFSA	1290	27
University of St. Thomas	MN	87	FAFSA	1250	29
Avila University	MO	73	FAFSA	1140	24
College of the Ozarks	MO	86	FAFSA	1260	25
Culver-Stockton College	MO	72	FAFSA	1060	23

Drury University	MO	76	FAFSA	1320	29
Lindenwood University	MO	94	FAFSA	1070	25
Maryville University of St. Louis	MO	74	FAFSA	1150	27
Northwest Missouri State University*	MO	78	FAFSA	1100	25
Rockhurst University	MO	94	FAFSA	1290	28
Truman State University*	MO	87	FAFSA	1370	30
University of Missouri -- Columbia*	MO	80	FAFSA	1310	28
University of Missouri--St. Louis*	MO	73	FAFSA	1210	27
Washington University in St. Louis	MO	100	CSS & NCP	1570	34
Westminster College	MO	92	FAFSA	1190	27
William Jewell College	MO	77	FAFSA	1190	28
Blue Mountain College	MS	82	FAFSA	1200	26
Millsaps College	MS	87	FAFSA	1270	29
Mississippi College	MS	82	FAFSA	1210	28
University of Mississippi*	MS	74	FAFSA	1180	27
Carroll College	MT	77	FAFSA	1200	27
Montana State University -- Bozeman*	MT	92	FAFSA	1260	28
Rocky Mountain College	MT	73	FAFSA	1130	26
University of Great Falls	MT	73	FAFSA	1050	22
Campbell University	NC	91	FAFSA	n/a	n/a
Catawba College	NC	78	FAFSA	1090	24
Chowan University	NC	73	FAFSA	900	17
Davidson College	NC	100	CSS & NCP	1440	32
Duke University	NC	100	CSS & NCP	1550	34
Fayetteville State University*	NC	78	FAFSA	960	21

Gardner-Webb University	NC	71	FAFSA	1120	25
Greensboro College	NC	94	FAFSA	980	20
Guilford College	NC	83	FAFSA	1170	26
Lees-McRae College	NC	70	FAFSA	1060	23
Lenoir-Rhyne University	NC	78	FAFSA	1090	24
Mars Hill University	NC	78	FAFSA	1030	22
Meredith College	NC	75	FAFSA	1130	25
Montreat College	NC	82	FAFSA	1080	24
North Carolina State University -- Raleigh*	NC	81	FAFSA	1330	31
The University of Mount Olive	NC	74	FAFSA	1070	22
University of North Carolina at Asheville*	NC	71	FAFSA	1290	28
University of North Carolina at Chapel Hill*	NC	100	CSS	1440	32
Wake Forest University	NC	99	CSS & NCP	1420	32
Warren Wilson College	NC	82	FAFSA	990	21
William Peace University	NC	85	FAFSA	990	21
Wingate University	NC	76	FAFSA	1110	23
Mayville State University*	ND	75	FAFSA	1040	22
Minot State University*	ND	71	FAFSA	1050	25
North Dakota State University*	ND	70	FAFSA	1370	26
University of Jamestown	ND	76	FAFSA	1130	25
Valley City State University*	ND	77	FAFSA	970	25
College of St. Mary	NE	78	FAFSA	1160	25
Concordia University, Nebraska	NE	81	FAFSA	1060	27
Creighton University	NE	85	FAFSA	1300	29
Doane College	NE	95	FAFSA	1160	25

Hastings College	NE	82	FAFSA	1130	27
Union College	NE	72	FAFSA	1160	25
University of Nebraska -- Lincoln*	NE	81	FAFSA	1300	28
Dartmouth College	NH	100	CSS & NCP	1550	34
Franklin Pierce University	NH	73	FAFSA	1050	22
New England College	NH	70	FAFSA	1000	23
Saint Anselm College	NH	83	CSS & NCP	1230	28
University of New Hampshire*	NH	79	FAFSA	1200	27
Caldwell University	NJ	76	FAFSA	1070	23
College of Saint Elizabeth	NJ	97	FAFSA	940	20
Felician College	NJ	76	FAFSA	960	21
Georgian Court University	NJ	78	FAFSA	1050	23
Kean University*	NJ	76	FAFSA	1000	22
Princeton University	NJ	100	CSS & NCP	1600	35
Rider University	NJ	75	FAFSA	1120	25
Rowan University*	NJ	84	FAFSA	1220	27
New Mexico Institute of Mining and Technology*	NM	80	FAFSA	1310	29
St. John's College	NM	92	CSS	1450	30
Alfred University	NY	87	FAFSA	1200	27
Bard College	NY	92	CSS & NCP	1390	32
Barnard College	NY	100	CSS & NCP	1440	32
Canisius College	NY	86	FAFSA	1180	27
Cazenovia College	NY	83	FAFSA	1060	24
Clarkson University	NY	90	FAFSA	1290	29

Colgate University	NY	100	CSS & NCP	1470	32
College of Mount St. Vincent	NY	71	FAFSA	1010	22
Columbia University	NY	100	CSS & NCP	1570	35
Cornell University	NY	100	CSS & NCP	1510	34
CUNY -- City College*	NY	84	FAFSA	1220	27
CUNY -- Hunter College*	NY	73	FAFSA	1270	29
CUNY -- John Jay College of Criminal Justice*	NY	85	FAFSA	1040	23
CUNY -- Queens College*	NY	95	FAFSA	1180	26
CUNY -- York College*	NY	99	FAFSA	1220	28
Elmira College	NY	77	CSS	1180	27
Fashion Institute of Technology*	NY	75	FAFSA	n/a	n/a
Fordham University	NY	80	CSS & NCP	1350	30
Hamilton College	NY	100	CSS & NCP	1470	33
Hartwick College	NY	80	FAFSA	1110	26
Hilbert College	NY	73	FAFSA	1030	23
Ithaca College	NY	90	CSS	1300	30
Juilliard School	NY	79	CSS	n/a	n/a
Keuka College	NY	70	FAFSA	1050	23
Le Moyne College	NY	80	FAFSA	1160	27
Manhattanville College	NY	71	FAFSA	1160	26
Nazareth College of Rochester	NY	83	FAFSA	1190	27
New York University	NY	72	CSS & NCP	1450	32
Niagara University	NY	85	FAFSA	1130	25
Pace University	NY	72	FAFSA	1170	26

Rensselaer Polytechnic Institute	NY	85	CSS	1490	32
Roberts Wesleyan College	NY	81	FAFSA	1160	26
Rochester Institute of Technology	NY	86	FAFSA	1320	31
Sarah Lawrence College	NY	90	CSS & NCP	1380	32
Siena College	NY	76	FAFSA	1220	27
Skidmore College	NY	100	CSS & NCP	1350	30
St. Bonaventure University	NY	84	FAFSA	1160	27
St. John Fisher College	NY	82	FAFSA	1160	27
St. John's University	NY	98	FAFSA	1210	28
St. Lawrence University	NY	86	CSS & NCP	1290	29
Stony Brook University*	NY	72	FAFSA	1350	30
SUNY -- College of Environmental Science and Forestry*	NY	82	FAFSA	1280	29
SUNY -- Oswego*	NY	86	FAFSA	1190	26
SUNY -- Plattsburgh*	NY	81	FAFSA	1160	25
SUNY -- Potsdam*	NY	90	FAFSA	1140	27
Syracuse University	NY	96	CSS & NCP	1280	29
The College at Brockport, SUNY*	NY	72	FAFSA	1150	25
The College of St. Rose	NY	78	FAFSA	1150	26
The Cooper Union	NY	91	CSS	1510	34
Touro College	NY	75	FAFSA	1180	25
Union College	NY	100	CSS & NCP	1400	31
University of Rochester	NY	97	CSS & NCP	1460	33
Utica College	NY	77	FAFSA	1070	24

Vassar College	NY	100	CSS & NCP	1490	33
Vaughn College of Aeronautics and Technology	NY	91	FAFSA	1090	24
Wagner College	NY	78	FAFSA	1270	27
Wells College	NY	84	FAFSA	1150	26
Yeshiva University	NY	92	FAFSA	1360	29
Baldwin Wallace University	OH	88	FAFSA	1180	25
Bluffton University	OH	92	FAFSA	1140	23
Bowling Green State University*	OH	74	FAFSA	1160	25
Capital University	OH	81	FAFSA	1200	27
Case Western Reserve University	OH	87	CSS & NCP	1470	33
Denison University	OH	97	FAFSA	1380	31
John Carroll University	OH	83	FAFSA	1200	27
Kenyon College	OH	94	CSS & NCP	1420	32
Lake Erie College	OH	74	FAFSA	1080	23
Malone University	OH	81	FAFSA	1110	25
Marietta College	OH	87	FAFSA	1220	27
Mount St. Joseph University	OH	82	FAFSA	1110	24
Oberlin College	OH	100	CSS	1450	32
Ohio Wesleyan University	OH	79	FAFSA	1220	28
The College of Wooster	OH	94	CSS	1320	30
The Ohio State University - - Columbus*	OH	71	FAFSA	1390	31
University of Dayton	OH	86	FAFSA	1250	29
University of Mount Union	OH	76	FAFSA	1130	25
University of Rio Grande	OH	82	FAFSA	1040	22
Ursuline College	OH	85	FAFSA	1170	25

Wittenberg University	OH	83	FAFSA	1250	28
Wright State University*	OH	70	FAFSA	1160	25
Xavier University	OH	74	FAFSA	1200	27
Northeastern State University*	OK	99	FAFSA	1120	24
Oklahoma Baptist University	OK	78	FAFSA	1220	30
Oklahoma Christian University	OK	78	FAFSA	1230	28
Oklahoma State University*	OK	78	FAFSA	1220	28
Oral Roberts University	OK	76	FAFSA	1130	26
Southwestern Oklahoma State University*	OK	93	FAFSA	1120	24
The University of Tulsa	OK	86	FAFSA	1400	32
University of Oklahoma*	OK	83	FAFSA	1340	29
University of Science and Arts of Oklahoma*	OK	74	FAFSA	1000	25
George Fox University	OR	87	FAFSA	1210	26
Lewis and Clark College	OR	88	CSS	1380	31
Linfield College	OR	85	FAFSA	1200	26
Northwest Christian University	OR	80	FAFSA	1100	24
Pacific University	OR	77	FAFSA	1200	27
Reed College	OR	100	CSS & NCP	1480	33
University of Portland	OR	72	FAFSA	1310	30
Warner Pacific College	OR	72	FAFSA	1030	21
Willamette University	OR	84	FAFSA	1320	29
Albright College	PA	83	FAFSA	1150	25
Allegheny College	PA	92	FAFSA	1250	29
Bryn Mawr College	PA	100	CSS & NCP	1440	32
Bucknell University	PA	91	CSS	1400	32

Cairn University	PA	75	FAFSA	1110	25
Carnegie Mellon University	PA	83	CSS & NCP	1540	34
Cedar Crest College	PA	77	FAFSA	1110	23
Chatham University	PA	80	FAFSA	1160	27
Chestnut Hill College	PA	71	FAFSA	1080	23
DeSales University	PA	71	FAFSA	1150	27
Dickinson College	PA	98	CSS & NCP	1370	31
Duquesne University	PA	84	FAFSA	1230	28
Eastern University	PA	74	FAFSA	1150	26
Elizabethtown College	PA	80	FAFSA	1240	28
Franklin & Marshall College	PA	100	CSS & NCP	1390	30
Gettysburg College	PA	90	CSS	1360	29
Haverford College	PA	100	CSS & NCP	1490	34
Holy Family University	PA	82	FAFSA	1020	22
Juniata College	PA	85	FAFSA	1250	32
Keystone College	PA	72	FAFSA	1030	22
King's College	PA	70	FAFSA	1140	26
La Roche College	PA	89	FAFSA	1040	23
Lafayette College	PA	99	CSS & NCP	1400	31
Lebanon Valley College	PA	80	FAFSA	1210	26
Lehigh University	PA	92	CSS & NCP	1410	32
Lock Haven University of Pennsylvania*	PA	86	FAFSA	1050	22
Mansfield University of Pennsylvania*	PA	99	FAFSA	1050	23
Marywood University	PA	78	FAFSA	1130	25
Messiah College	PA	74	FAFSA	1240	27

Millersville University of Pennsylvania*	PA	79	FAFSA	1120	23
Misericordia University	PA	77	FAFSA	1170	26
Moravian College	PA	75	FAFSA	1130	26
Muhlenberg College	PA	92	CSS & NCP	1330	31
Philadelphia University	PA	75	FAFSA	1180	26
Point Park University	PA	72	FAFSA	1100	24
Robert Morris University	PA	74	FAFSA	1150	26
Rosemont College	PA	88	FAFSA	1070	22
Saint Francis University	PA	72	FAFSA	1130	25
Saint Joseph's University	PA	76	FAFSA	1220	27
Saint Vincent College	PA	83	FAFSA	1160	25
Seton Hill University	PA	77	FAFSA	1170	27
Susquehanna University	PA	82	CSS	1210	28
Swarthmore College	PA	100	CSS & NCP	1540	34
Temple University*	PA	70	FAFSA	1230	28
Thiel College	PA	71	FAFSA	1060	23
University of Pennsylvania	PA	100	CSS & NCP	1550	34
Ursinus College	PA	83	FAFSA	1260	28
Villanova University	PA	81	CSS & NCP	1400	31
Washington & Jefferson College	PA	83	FAFSA	1230	28
Waynesburg University	PA	80	FAFSA	1100	26
Westminster College	PA	76	FAFSA	1190	27
Widener University	PA	81	FAFSA	1130	24
Wilkes University	PA	75	FAFSA	1180	26
Brown University	RI	100	CSS & NCP	1550	34
Providence College	RI	88	CSS	1250	28

Rhode Island College*	RI	72	FAFSA	1050	21
Roger Williams University	RI	83	CSS	1200	27
Salve Regina University	RI	75	FAFSA	1180	27
Anderson University	SC	71	FAFSA	1170	26
Coker College	SC	71	FAFSA	1070	24
Columbia College	SC	83	FAFSA	1140	25
Converse College	SC	70	FAFSA	1150	25
Furman University	SC	80	CSS	1340	30
Presbyterian College	SC	87	FAFSA	1210	26
Wofford College	SC	85	FAFSA	1270	30
Augustana University	SD	98	FAFSA	1290	28
Dakota State University*	SD	75	FAFSA	1170	26
Dakota Wesleyan University	SD	80	FAFSA	1220	27
Mount Marty College	SD	92	FAFSA	1090	23
Northern State University*	SD	75	FAFSA	1120	25
South Dakota School of Mines and Technology*	SD	78	FAFSA	1310	28
University of South Dakota*	SD	78	FAFSA	1050	25
Carson-Newman University	TN	84	FAFSA	1150	26
Fisk University	TN	85	CSS & NCP	1110	23
King University	TN	79	FAFSA	1050	25
Lincoln Memorial University	TN	76	FAFSA	1024	24
Maryville College	TN	75	FAFSA	1090	26
Middle Tennessee State University*	TN	70	FAFSA	1190	25
Milligan College	TN	82	FAFSA	1170	26
Rhodes College	TN	93	CSS & NCP	1380	31

Sewanee: The University of the South	TN	95	CSS & NCP	1360	30
University of Memphis*	TN	77	FAFSA	1150	26
University of Tennessee at Chattanooga*	TN	74	FAFSA	1180	26
University of Tennessee at Martin*	TN	77	FAFSA	1160	25
Vanderbilt University	TN	100	CSS	1580	34
Angelo State University*	TX	91	FAFSA	1070	24
Austin College	TX	85	FAFSA	1320	27
Concordia University Texas	TX	80	FAFSA	1110	25
Houston Baptist University	TX	73	FAFSA	1160	25
Howard Payne University	TX	78	FAFSA	1070	23
LeTourneau University	TX	74	FAFSA	1310	30
Lubbock Christian University	TX	70	FAFSA	1110	25
Our Lady of the Lake University	TX	78	FAFSA	1030	22
Prairie View A&M University*	TX	87	FAFSA	940	19
Rice University	TX	100	CSS & NCP	1550	34
Schreiner University	TX	74	FAFSA	1090	24
Southern Methodist University	TX	88	CSS & NCP	1400	31
Southwestern University	TX	90	FAFSA	1260	28
St. Edward's University	TX	74	FAFSA	1210	27
Texas A&M University -- College Station*	TX	74	FAFSA	1310	30
Texas A&M University -- Commerce*	TX	76	FAFSA	1050	22
Texas Lutheran University	TX	84	FAFSA	1120	23
Texas State University -- San Marcos*	TX	81	FAFSA	1150	25

Texas Tech University*	TX	76	FAFSA	1200	27
Texas Wesleyan University	TX	76	FAFSA	1090	23
Texas Woman's University*	TX	84	FAFSA	1060	24
The University of Texas at Austin*	TX	77	FAFSA	1390	31
The University of Texas of the Permian Basin*	TX	74	FAFSA	1070	22
Trinity University	TX	99	CSS	1360	31
University of Dallas	TX	82	FAFSA	1320	30
University of North Texas*	TX	72	FAFSA	1210	26
University of Texas at Arlington*	TX	76	FAFSA	1200	26
University of Texas at Dallas*	TX	76	FAFSA	1370	31
University of the Incarnate Word	TX	76	FAFSA	1070	23
Westminster College	UT	83	FAFSA	1190	27
Bridgewater College	VA	87	FAFSA	1140	27
College of William and Mary*	VA	74	CSS	1470	33
Emory & Henry College	VA	93	FAFSA	1120	25
Ferrum College	VA	82	FAFSA	980	22
Hampden-Sydney College	VA	80	FAFSA	1210	27
Hollins University	VA	86	FAFSA	1210	30
Lynchburg College	VA	83	FAFSA	1090	24
Mary Baldwin College	VA	73	FAFSA	1090	24
Radford University*	VA	79	FAFSA	1060	22
Randolph College	VA	83	FAFSA	1200	29
Randolph-Macon College	VA	83	FAFSA	1190	26
Roanoke College	VA	80	FAFSA	1200	27
Sweet Briar College	VA	80	FAFSA	1160	28
University of Richmond	VA	100	CSS & NCP	1430	32

University of Virginia*	VA	100	CSS	1460	33
University of Virginia -- Wise*	VA	96	FAFSA	1050	23
Virginia Military Institute*	VA	89	FAFSA	1250	28
Virginia Wesleyan College	VA	70	FAFSA	1100	25
Washington and Lee University	VA	100	CSS & NCP	1460	33
Bennington College	VT	77	CSS & NCP	1400	32
Green Mountain College	VT	78	FAFSA	1120	24
Marlboro College	VT	76	FAFSA	1370	28
Middlebury College	VT	100	CSS & NCP	1470	33
Norwich University	VT	76	FAFSA	1160	26
Saint Michael's College	VT	82	FAFSA	1250	28
University of Vermont*	VT	70	FAFSA	1290	29
Central Washington University*	WA	88	FAFSA	1080	24
Gonzaga University	WA	80	FAFSA	1290	29
Northwest University	WA	78	FAFSA	1140	25
Pacific Lutheran University	WA	90	FAFSA	1210	29
Seattle Pacific University	WA	82	FAFSA	1230	27
St. Martin's University	WA	82	FAFSA	1160	28
University of Puget Sound	WA	75	FAFSA	1330	30
University of Washington, Bothell*	WA	81	FAFSA	1140	24
University of Washington, Seattle*	WA	82	FAFSA	1350	31
University of Washington, Tacoma*	WA	81	FAFSA	1090	23
Walla Walla University	WA	90	FAFSA	1230	26
Western Washington University*	WA	88	FAFSA	1210	27
Whitman College	WA	93	CSS & NCP	1430	32

Whitworth University	WA	81	FAFSA	1280	29
Beloit College	WI	93	FAFSA	1370	30
Cardinal Stritch University	WI	78	FAFSA	1000	24
Carroll University	WI	87	FAFSA	1200	26
Concordia University Wisconsin	WI	79	FAFSA	1170	26
Edgewood College	WI	79	FAFSA	980	25
Lawrence University	WI	93	CSS & NCP	1410	31
Marian University Wisconsin	WI	72	FAFSA	1090	23
Marquette University	WI	76	FAFSA	1290	29
Milwaukee School of Engineering	WI	82	FAFSA	1350	30
Mount Mary University	WI	80	FAFSA	1050	22
Northland College	WI	86	FAFSA	1180	26
St. Norbert College	WI	84	FAFSA	1240	27
University of Wisconsin -- Eau Claire*	WI	85	FAFSA	1310	26
University of Wisconsin -- Green Bay*	WI	71	FAFSA	1160	25
University of Wisconsin -- Madison*	WI	78	FAFSA	1410	32
University of Wisconsin -- Stout*	WI	84	FAFSA	1130	24
University of Wisconsin -- Superior*	WI	80	FAFSA	1130	24
Wisconsin Lutheran College	WI	81	FAFSA	1210	26
Alderson-Broaddus University	WV	80	FAFSA	1050	24
Concord University*	WV	91	FAFSA	1060	24
Davis & Elkins College	WV	79	FAFSA	1040	26
Fairmont State University*	WV	72	FAFSA	1020	23
Shepherd University*	WV	82	FAFSA	1090	24

West Virginia University*	WV	72	FAFSA	1140	26
West Virginia University Institute of Technology*	WV	72	FAFSA	1080	24
West Virginia Wesleyan College	WV	90	FAFSA	1060	25
Wheeling Jesuit University	WV	85	FAFSA	1110	25

Chapter 6: How To Get Money Based On Your Achievements

"Charm strikes the sight, but merit wins the soul."
— Alexander Pope

If your Expected Family Contribution (EFC) is too high, there are schools that award money based on grades and test scores. At these top schools, even slightly above average grades and SAT, ACT, and SAT Subject Test scores qualify you to receive huge chunks of money from their endowment funds. Before you decide it's time to apply to schools based on merit, you should be sure your EFC is indeed too high and that you've taken all the steps to minimize it. Make sure you're doing this with help, so you're not doing anything counterproductive.

Not every college offers merit scholarships. For instance, Ivy League colleges do not offer merit scholarships because virtually each of their students would qualify. However, if your student is "Ivy League Material," they can easily command a very large merit scholarship at almost any other college in the country. Many parents don't realize that most prestigious colleges in America do offer merit scholarships, and sometimes these colleges are among the top 25 or even top ten for a specific major.

There are two types of merit scholarships. The first type of merit scholarship requires an additional application and has a special (and usually early) deadline. The other type of merit scholarship does not require an additional application other than an application for general admission. You must understand which school requires an additional application submitted early to compete for a merit scholarship and which do not, so that you do not miss a very valuable deadline and leave a lot of money on the table. You and your child must also have a working list of prospective colleges in order to see when and how each college reviews their merit candidates.

The best way to find out if a college offers a merit scholarship is to visit the college's financial aid page and search for "Scholarships," "Types of Aid" or "Merit Scholarships" to see the deadlines, minimum qualifications and preferred qualifications. Look for this as soon as possible—even if your child is a freshman. It doesn't hurt to know what GPA, scores and attributes your child should have to ensure they qualify for a merit scholarship for at least one college on their college list.

Take Tulane University for example. Their website mentions scholarships that have special deadlines and require additional materials as well as merit scholarships that do not. These scholarships are given to some of the top students who apply to their college every year.

Here is an excerpt from Tulane's Scholarship site:

"**Merit-based Scholarships:** All freshmen applicants are considered for partial merit scholarships ranging from $10,000 to $30,000 per year. Additionally, there are four merit scholarships that require supplemental materials and have special application procedures: the Deans' Honors Scholarship, The Paul Tulane Award, The Stamps-Tulane Scholarship and The Community Service Scholarship.

Full tuition scholarships, The Dean's Honor Scholarship and The Paul Tulane Award: Students applying for the DHS or The Paul Tulane Award must apply either Early Action or Single Choice Early Action and submit the application for admission and all supporting materials by November 15th; DHS and Paul Tulane Award application materials are then due by December 15th."

Another good school for a merit scholarship is Oklahoma University. They post the SAT/ACT and GPA requirements for their biggest out-of-state scholarships in a PDF right on their website.

SCHOLARSHIP	DESCRIPTION	AMOUNT	ELIGIBILITY
National Merit Scholars	Combination of state, university and National Merit funding.	$124,000	Guaranteed to every National Merit Finalist who names OU as his/her college choice prior to May 1.
Oklahoma State Regents' Institutional Nominee	Partial tuition waiver plus cash award from state over four years.	$43,200	Minimum qualifying criteria and award amount set annually by the State Regents in late fall.
Award of Excellence	Partial tuition waiver over four years.	$32,000	31 ACT or 1360 SAT* (or greater) and 3.75 GPA or top 10% class rank
Distinguished Scholar	Partial tuition waiver over four years	$28,000	29-30 ACT or 1290-1350 SAT* ($7,000 x 4 years) and 3.75 GPA or top 10% class rank
University Scholar	Partial tuition waiver over four years.	$24,000	28 ACT or 1250-1280 SAT* (and 3.5 GPA or top 10% class rank
Academic Achievement Award	Partial tuition waiver over four years.	$20,000	26-27 ACT or 1170-1240 SAT* and 3.5 GPA

*SAT = Critical Reading plus Math (writing score is excluded)

The bottom line with merit scholarship is if you're a student that has good grades and test scores and you're willing to apply to a school that could give you a lot of money, it's helpful to create a short list of colleges you're interested in and do some research to see what they have to offer and who they are willing to give money to attend. Even if your child is in middle school or is a freshman in high school, it is very helpful to know that they will need to have a 31 ACT score along with a 3.75 GPA, for example to command an $8,000 per year scholarship to attend Oklahoma University. By knowing this early, you will have enough time to give your child the resources needed to achieve these marks.

This next list shows you colleges that offer full-ride scholarships to their top applicants. If you have a child with very competitive grades, test scores, extracurricular activities, and such, they should apply to a few of these colleges by the merit scholarship deadline.

These Colleges Offer Full Scholarships To Their Top Students:

Note: You can visit the websites and contact the admissions, financial aid and scholarship offices of each of these colleges to get more information on the particular scholarships they offer, as well as how to qualify and apply. In general, you need to be in the top 1-2% of their applicants to compete, but if you apply and get the scholarship, you will pay little to no money out-of-pocket to attend these schools. This list is most appropriate for the student who has extraordinary grades and test scores and whose parents' EFC is too high to get Need-based financial aid.

This is not the list for students whose grades and test scores are average or below average at the schools they are applying to. Students with average or below average grades and test scores should apply to schools that offer Need-based grants and partial merit scholarships. The list of schools for a less competitive merit candidate will be under "Here is a list of colleges that tend to give out at least $40,000 in scholarship money over 4 years to their top applicants regardless of your income & assets:"

Colleges That Offer Full Ride Scholarships
Agnes Scott College
Arcadia University
Boston College
Boston University
Carthage College
Catholic University
Centre College
Clark University
Clemson University
Davidson College

Denison University
Duke University
Emory University
Fordham University
Furman University
Georgia Institute of Technology
Georgia Southern University
Hendrix College
Hofstra University
Howard University
Illinois Institute of Technology
Indiana University
Johns Hopkins University
Knox College
Louisiana State University
Maryville University
Miami University
Michigan State University
Mississippi State University
Missouri State University
North Carolina A&T State University
North Carolina State University
Northeastern University
Ohio State University
Rhodes College
Rutgers University
Saint Louis University
Scripps College
Southern Methodist University
Southwestern University
Stevens Institute of Technology
Syracuse University

Temple University
Texas A&M University
Texas Christian University
Tulane University
University of Alabama
University of Buffalo
University of Delaware
University of Georgia
University of Houston
University of Illinois
University of Kentucky
University of Louisville
University of Maryland
University of Miami
University of Mississippi (Ole Miss)
University of New Mexico
University of North Carolina
University of North Carolina – Charlotte
University of North Carolina – Greensboro
University of Notre Dame
University of Pittsburgh
University of Richmond
University of Rochester
University of South Carolina
University of Southern California
University of Texas at Austin

I've compiled the list on the following few pages for any parent whose EFC is over $45,000 per year. Families in this category should invest in getting their child a high SAT or ACT score in order to make sure that their child's SAT/ACT scores are in the 25% percentile at the schools their child will apply to. There are many websites that can show you with reasonable accuracy the SAT or ACT scores of students who were accepted to almost any college. A good website to use is collegeboard.org. On this website you can search a college and view a breakdown of a college's student body's SAT or ACT scores grouped by bottom 25%, Middle 50% and top 25%. The numbers you want to pay attention to are the scores of the students in the top 25% of SAT and/or ACT scores. For instance, at Ohio Wesleyan University, the SAT scores of the top 25% of admitted students were 620 for Critical Reading, 630 for Math and 610 for Writing. This means that your student must have over an 1860 to have a fair shot of receiving at least $10,000 in scholarship money from Ohio Wesleyan University. Generally the higher the student's score is above the school's 25 percentile, the more money they will receive.

Just recently I had a student with an 1800 SAT score apply to Ohio Wesleyan University Early Action, and in less than 30 days she was offered a $100,000 scholarship over 4 years. She received this acceptance and merit scholarship offer before we even completed her financial aid forms. Once we submit her financial aid forms, I estimate she will receive close to $44,000 per year in financial aid per year if she attends OWU.

You Can Get $40,000 to $280,000 From These Colleges Regardless Of Your Income & Assets:

Note: On the right side of each college is the target SAT (Math and Critical Reading only) and ACT score to get the maximum scholarship amount. If your score is a few points below, you may still get a merit scholarship offer. The list is also sorted by most to least competitive merit scholarship pool. Each school will give out at least $40,000 over 4 years if you're a top candidate—sometimes a lot more. Be sure to ask is there's a special deadline or separate application for the scholarship and be sure to apply to a few colleges. As a general rule, you should push for an SAT score for at least a 1250 (Math and Critical Reading) or a 28 on the ACT to get a good scholarship to a good school.

College	City	State	Target SAT	Target ACT
Vanderbilt University	Nashville	TN	1600	36
Washington University in St. Louis	St. Louis	MO	1600	36
Duke University	Durham	NC	1600	36
Rice University	Houston	TX	1600	36
Franklin W. Olin College of Engineering	Needham	MA	1600	36
Carnegie Mellon University	Pittsburgh	PA	1590	36
Johns Hopkins University	Baltimore	MD	1580	36
University of Notre Dame	Notre Dame	IN	1570	36

Cooper Union for the Advancement of Science and Art	New York	NY	1560	36
Northeastern University	Boston	MA	1550	36
Claremont McKenna College	Claremont	CA	1570	35
Grinnell College	Grinnell	IA	1550	35
University of Southern California	Los Angeles	CA	1530	35
Brandeis University	Waltham	MA	1530	35
Case Western Reserve University	Cleveland	OH	1520	35
College of William and Mary	Williamsburg	VA	1520	35
Washington and Lee University	Lexington	VA	1510	35
Boston College	Chestnut Hill	MA	1510	35
Scripps College	Claremont	CA	1510	35
University of Rochester	Rochester	NY	1510	35
Rensselaer Polytechnic Institute	Troy	NY	1540	34
Macalester College	St. Paul	MN	1520	34
Emory University	Atlanta	GA	1510	34
Oberlin College	Oberlin	OH	1500	34
Davidson College	Davidson	NC	1490	34
St. John's College	Annapolis	MD	1490	34
Bryn Mawr College	Bryn Mawr	PA	1490	34
University of Richmond	Richmond	VA	1480	34
Whitman College	Walla Walla	WA	1480	34
Wake Forest University	Winston Salem	NC	1470	34
University of Miami	Coral Gables	FL	1470	34
Kenyon College	Gambier	OH	1470	34
Tulane University	New Orleans	LA	1460	34
Lehigh University	Bethlehem	PA	1460	34

Worcester Polytechnic Institute	Worcester	MA	1460	34
The University of Tulsa	Tulsa	OK	1450	34
Bennington College	Bennington	VT	1450	34
Bucknell University	Lewisburg	PA	1450	34
Bard College	Annandale on Hudson	NY	1440	34
St. Olaf College	Northfield	MN	1440	34
Santa Clara University	Santa Clara	CA	1440	34
Juniata College	Huntingdon	PA	1300	34
Smith College	Northampton	MA	1520	33
Mount Holyoke College	South Hadley	MA	1500	33
Lawrence University	Appleton	WI	1460	33
Boston University	Boston	MA	1460	33
Lafayette College	Easton	PA	1450	33
Southern Methodist University	Dallas	TX	1450	33
Bard College at Simon's Rock	Great Barrington	MA	1450	33
Villanova University	Villanova	PA	1450	33
The George Washington University	Washington	DC	1440	33
Occidental College	Los Angeles	CA	1440	33
College of the Holy Cross	Worcester	MA	1430	33
Denison University	Granville	OH	1430	33
Illinois Institute of Technology	Chicago	IL	1430	33
Rhodes College	Memphis	TN	1430	33
Lewis and Clark College	Portland	OR	1430	33
Earlham College	Richmond	IN	1420	33
University of Texas at Dallas	Richardson	TX	1420	33

Trinity University	San Antonio	TX	1410	33
University of Pittsburgh	Pittsburgh	PA	1410	33
Centre College	Danville	KY	1390	33
Clark University	Worcester	MA	1380	33
Muhlenberg College	Allentown	PA	1380	33
Hendrix College	Conway	AR	1370	33
The University of Alabama	Tuscaloosa	AL	1300	33
Patrick Henry College	Purcellville	VA	1450	32
Kalamazoo College	Kalamazoo	MI	1430	32
Illinois Wesleyan University	Bloomington	IL	1430	32
University of California, Santa Barbara	Santa Barbara	CA	1430	32
Babson College	Babson Park	MA	1420	32
Beloit College	Beloit	WI	1420	32
Knox College	Galesburg	IL	1410	32
Sewanee: The University of the South	Sewanee	TN	1410	32
Milwaukee School of Engineering	Milwaukee	WI	1400	32
Skidmore College	Saratoga Springs	NY	1400	32
Fordham University	Bronx	NY	1400	32
Trinity College	Hartford	CT	1390	32
Furman University	Greenville	SC	1390	32
American University	Washington	DC	1390	32
College of the Atlantic	Bar Harbor	MN	1390	32
Pepperdine University	Malibu	CA	1380	32
Bentley University	Waltham	MA	1380	32
Emerson College	Boston	MA	1380	32
Baylor University	Waco	TX	1380	32

University of Puget Sound	Tacoma	WA	1380	32
The College of Wooster	Wooster	OH	1370	32
University of Dallas	Irving	TX	1370	32
University of San Diego	San Diego	CA	1370	32
University of Portland	Portland	OR	1360	32
Drake University	Des Moines	IA	1360	32
LeTourneau University	Longview	TX	1360	32
University of the Pacific	Stockton	CA	1360	32
University of Denver	Denver	CO	1350	32
Transylvania University	Lexington	KY	1350	32
John Brown University	Siloam Springs	AR	1340	32
Texas Christian University	Fort Worth	TX	1330	32
Butler University	Indianapolis	IN	1330	32
Florida Institute of Technology	Melbourne	FL	1320	32
Wofford College	Spartanburg	SC	1320	32
Taylor University	Upland	IN	1310	32
Oklahoma Baptist University	Shawnee	OK	1270	32
Hollins University	Roanoke	VA	1260	32
Yeshiva University	New York	NY	1410	31
Gettysburg College	Gettysburg	PA	1410	31
Hampshire College	Amherst	MA	1400	31
Agnes Scott College	Decatur	GA	1380	31
Cornell College	Mount Vernon	IA	1370	31
Willamette University	Salem	OR	1370	31
Kettering University	Flint	MI	1360	31
Cedarville University	Cedarville	OH	1350	31
DePauw University	Greencastle	IN	1350	31

Creighton University	Omaha	NE	1350	31
New Jersey Institute of Technology	Newark	NJ	1350	31
Ithaca College	Ithaca	NY	1350	31
Clarkson University	Potsdam	NY	1340	31
St. Lawrence University	Canton	NY	1340	31
Mercer University	Macon	GA	1340	31
Chapman University	Orange	CA	1340	31
Westmont College	Santa Barbara	CA	1340	31
Gonzaga University	Spokane	WA	1340	31
Marquette University	Milwaukee	WI	1340	31
University of Vermont	Burlington	VT	1340	31
Rollins College	Winter Park	FL	1330	31
Whitworth University	Spokane	WA	1330	31
Goucher College	Baltimore	MD	1330	31
Gordon College	Wenham	MA	1330	31
Covenant College	Lookout Mountain	GA	1330	31
Seattle University	Seattle	WA	1330	31
Millsaps College	Jackson	MS	1320	31
Washington College	Chestertown	MD	1320	31
Loyola University Maryland	Baltimore	MD	1320	31
Augustana College	Rock Island	IL	1310	31
Loyola University Chicago	Chicago	IL	1310	31
Berry College	Mount Berry	GA	1310	31
Lipscomb University	Nashville	TN	1310	31
College of Saint Benedict	St. Joseph	MN	1300	31
University of St. Thomas	St. Paul	MN	1300	31

Allegheny College	Meadville	PA	1300	31
Mills College	Oakland	CA	1300	31
University of Dayton	Dayton	OH	1300	31
Dordt College	Sioux Center	IA	1290	31
University of Evansville	Evansville	IN	1290	31
Eckerd College	St. Petersburg	FL	1290	31
Aquinas College	Nashville	TN	1290	31
Nova Southeastern University	Ft. Lauderdale	FL	1290	31
Samford University	Birmingham	AL	1290	31
Principia College	Elsah	IL	1280	31
Valparaiso University	Valparaiso	IN	1270	31
Pacific Lutheran University	Tacoma	WA	1260	31
Randolph College	Lynchburg	VA	1250	31
Marlboro College	Marlboro	VT	1420	30
Wheaton College	Norton	MA	1400	30
Concordia College -- Moorhead	Moorhead	MN	1380	30
Oklahoma City University	Oklahoma City	OK	1350	30
Rockhurst University	Kansas City	MO	1340	30
Pratt Institute	Brooklyn	NY	1340	30
Coe College	Cedar Rapids	IA	1330	30
Stetson University	Deland	FL	1330	30
Augustana University	Sioux Falls	SD	1330	30
Bethel University	St. Paul	MN	1330	30
DePaul University	Chicago	IL	1320	30
Ursinus College	Collegeville	PA	1310	30
Southwestern University	Georgetown	TX	1310	30
Fairfield University	Fairfield	CT	1310	30

Goshen College	Goshen	IN	1310	30
Simmons College	Boston	MA	1310	30
Albany College of Pharmacy and Health Sciences	Albany	NY	1310	30
Wabash College	Crawfordsville	IN	1300	30
Wittenberg University	Springfield	OH	1300	30
Luther College	Decorah	IA	1300	30
Lake Forest College	Lake Forest	IL	1300	30
Saint Michael's College	Colchester	VT	1300	30
Providence College	Providence	RI	1300	30
University of San Francisco	San Francisco	CA	1300	30
Elizabethtown College	Elizabethtown	PA	1290	30
Bryant University	Smithfield	RI	1290	30
Asbury University	Wilmore	KY	1290	30
Oglethorpe University	Atlanta	GA	1280	30
Hofstra University	Hempstead	NY	1280	30
Washington & Jefferson College	Washington	PA	1280	30
Catholic University of America	Washington	DC	1280	30
Lawrence Technological University	Southfield	MI	1280	30
Loyola University New Orleans	New Orleans	LA	1280	30
Saint Anselm College	Manchester	NH	1280	30
Duquesne University	Pittsburgh	PA	1280	30
Sacred Heart University	Fairfield	CT	1280	30
Ohio Wesleyan University	Delaware	OH	1270	30
Florida Southern College	Lakeland	FL	1270	30

Saint John's University	Collegeville	MN	1270	30
Stonehill College	Easton	MA	1270	30
St. John's University	Queens	NY	1260	30
Susquehanna University	Selinsgrove	PA	1260	30
Saint Mary's College	Notre Dame	IN	1260	30
VanderCook College of Music	Chicago	IL	1250	30
William Jewell College	Liberty	MO	1240	30
Centenary College of Louisiana	Shreveport	LA	1230	30
Hanover College	Hanover	IN	1220	30
Sweet Briar College	Sweet Briar	VA	1210	30
St. Martin's University	Lacey	WA	1210	30
Austin College	Sherman	TX	1370	29
Alma College	Alma	MI	1370	29
Wagner College	Staten Island	NY	1320	29
University of the Sciences in Philadelphia	Philadelphia	PA	1310	29
Webster University	St. Louis	MO	1300	29
St. Norbert College	De Pere	WI	1300	29
Simpson College	Indianola	IA	1290	29
North Central College	Naperville	IL	1290	29
Messiah College	Mechanicsburg	PA	1290	29
Westminster College	Salt Lake City	UT	1290	29
Northwestern College	Orange City	IA	1290	29
Seattle Pacific University	Seattle	WA	1280	29
Hamline University	St. Paul	MN	1280	29
College of Charleston	Charleston	SC	1280	29
The College of St. Scholastica	Duluth	MN	1270	29

109

Dakota Wesleyan University	Mitchell	SD	1270	29
University of St. Thomas	Houston	TX	1270	29
Marietta College	Marietta	OH	1270	29
Wentworth Institute of Technology	Boston	MA	1270	29
Saint Joseph's University	Philadelphia	PA	1270	29
Andrews University	Berrien Springs	MI	1270	29
Albion College	Albion	MI	1260	29
St. Edward's University	Austin	TX	1260	29
Hampden-Sydney College	Hampden-Sydney	VA	1260	29
Quinnipiac University	Hamden	CT	1260	29
St. Mary's College of California	Moraga	CA	1260	29
University of Scranton	Scranton	PA	1260	29
Spring Hill College	Mobile	AL	1250	29
Capital University	Columbus	OH	1250	29
John Carroll University	University Heights	OH	1250	29
McDaniel College	Westminster	MD	1250	29
Kansas City Art Institute	Kansas City	MO	1250	29
Pacific University	Forest Grove	OR	1250	29
California Lutheran University	Thousand Oaks	CA	1250	29
Roanoke College	Salem	VA	1250	29
Xavier University	Cincinnati	OH	1250	29
Carroll College	Helena	MT	1250	29
Roger Williams University	Bristol	RI	1250	29
Nazareth College of Rochester	Rochester	NY	1240	29

110

The College of Idaho	Caldwell	ID	1240	29
Westminster College	Fulton	MO	1240	29
Regis University	Denver	CO	1240	29
Abilene Christian University	Abilene	TX	1240	29
Manhattan College	Riverdale	NY	1240	29
Elmira College	Elmira	NY	1230	29
Bellarmine University	Louisville	KY	1230	29
Canisius College	Buffalo	NY	1230	29
Salve Regina University	Newport	RI	1230	29
Savannah College of Art and Design	Savannah	GA	1230	29
Trinity Christian College	Palos Heights	IL	1230	29
Seton Hill University	Greensburg	PA	1220	29
Chatham University	Pittsburgh	PA	1210	29
St. Bonaventure University	St. Bonaventure	NY	1210	29
Trine University	Angola	IN	1210	29
St. John Fisher College	Rochester	NY	1210	29
Palm Beach Atlantic University	West Palm Beach	FL	1210	29
Georgetown College	Georgetown	KY	1200	29
DeSales University	Center Valley	PA	1200	29
Maryville University of St. Louis	St. Louis	MO	1200	29
Bridgewater College	Bridgewater	VA	1190	29
Hastings College	Hastings	NE	1180	29
Central College	Pella	IA	1160	29
Sierra Nevada College	Incline Village	NV	1150	29
Concordia University, Nebraska	Seward	NE	1110	29

111

University of Detroit Mercy	Detroit	MI	1360	28
Minneapolis College of Art and Design	Minneapolis	MN	1300	28
Elmhurst College	Elmhurst	IL	1280	28
St. Catherine University	St. Paul	MN	1280	28
California College of the Arts	San Francisco	CA	1280	28
Lebanon Valley College	Annville	PA	1260	28
Carroll University	Waukesha	WI	1260	28
Aquinas College	Grand Rapids	MI	1260	28
Morningside College	Sioux City	IA	1260	28
George Fox University	Newberg	OR	1260	28
Wisconsin Lutheran College	Milwaukee	WI	1260	28
Linfield College	McMinnville	OR	1250	28
Assumption College	Worcester	MA	1250	28
Ramapo College of New Jersey	Mahwah	NJ	1250	28
Loras College	Dubuque	IA	1240	28
Randolph-Macon College	Ashland	VA	1240	28
Emmanuel College	Boston	MA	1240	28
Millikin University	Decatur	IL	1240	28
Northland College	Ashland	WI	1230	28
Wilkes University	Wilkes-Barre	PA	1230	28
New York Institute of Technology	Old Westbury	NY	1230	28
Philadelphia University	Philadelphia	PA	1230	28
Northwest Nazarene University	Nampa	ID	1230	28
Pace University	New York	NY	1220	28
Guilford College	Greensboro	NC	1220	28

Western New England University	Springfield	MA	1220	28
Misericordia University	Dallas	PA	1220	28
Concordia University Wisconsin	Mequon	WI	1220	28
St. Mary's University of Minnesota	Winona	MN	1210	28
Norwich University	Northfield	VT	1210	28
University of New Haven	West Haven	CT	1210	28
Queens University of Charlotte	Charlotte	NC	1210	28
Roberts Wesleyan College	Rochester	NY	1210	28
Wells College	Aurora	NY	1200	28
The College of St. Rose	Albany	NY	1200	28
Robert Morris University	Moon Township	PA	1200	28
King's College	Wilkes-Barre	PA	1190	28
Huntington University	Huntington	IN	1190	28
Wartburg College	Waverly	IA	1180	28
Moravian College	Bethlehem	PA	1180	28
Marywood University	Scranton	PA	1180	28
Rocky Mountain College	Billings	MT	1180	28
Oral Roberts University	Tulsa	OK	1180	28
Hartwick College	Oneonta	NY	1160	28
Baker University	Baldwin City	KS	1160	28
Maryville College	Maryville	TN	1140	28
Illinois College	Jacksonville	IL	1140	28
Regis College	Weston	MA	1110	28
Davis & Elkins College	Elkins	WV	1090	28
College of the Ozarks	Point Lookout	MO	1310	27

Columbus College of Art and Design	Columbus	OH	1250	27
Cornerstone University	Grand Rapids	MI	1240	27
Monmouth College	Monmouth	IL	1230	27
Baldwin Wallace University	Berea	OH	1230	27
McKendree University	Lebanon	IL	1230	27
The Citadel	Charleston	SC	1230	27
University of Wisconsin -- Platteville	Platteville	WI	1220	27
Whittier College	Whittier	CA	1220	27
College of St. Mary	Omaha	NE	1220	27
Mount Mercy University	Cedar Rapids	IA	1220	27
Mount Marty College	Yankton	SD	1220	27
Buena Vista University	Storm Lake	IA	1210	27
Saint Vincent College	Latrobe	PA	1210	27
Houston Baptist University	Houston	TX	1210	27
Concordia University -- Chicago	River Forest	IL	1210	27
Westminster College	New Wilmington	PA	1200	27
Albright College	Reading	PA	1200	27
Otis College of Art and Design	Los Angeles	CA	1200	27
Hood College	Frederick	MD	1190	27
Columbia College	Columbia	SC	1190	27
Lewis University	Romeoville	IL	1190	27
Hardin-Simmons University	Abilene	TX	1190	27
Saint Francis University	Loretto	PA	1180	27
Niagara University	Niagara University	NY	1180	27
Meredith College	Raleigh	NC	1180	27

Suffolk University	Boston	MA	1180	27
University of Mount Union	Alliance	OH	1180	27
Rider University	Lawrenceville	NJ	1170	27
Emory & Henry College	Emory	VA	1170	27
Merrimack College	North Andover	MA	1170	27
University of Indianapolis	Indianapolis	IN	1170	27
Iona College	New Rochelle	NY	1160	27
Jacksonville University	Jacksonville	FL	1160	27
Concordia University Texas	Austin	TX	1160	27
Malone University	Canton	OH	1160	27
University of Hartford	West Hartford	CT	1160	27
Virginia Wesleyan College	Norfolk	VA	1150	27
Franklin College	Franklin	IN	1150	27
Wheeling Jesuit University	Wheeling	WV	1150	27
The Sage Colleges	Troy	NY	1140	27
West Virginia Wesleyan College	Buckhannon	WV	1110	27
King University	Bristol	TN	1100	27
Tennessee Wesleyan College	Athens	TN	1070	27
Quincy University	Quincy	IL	1030	27
University of Findlay	Findlay	OH	1220	27
Adelphi University	Garden City	NY	1270	26
Mercyhurst University	Erie	PA	1260	26
Muskingum University	New Concord	OH	1230	26
Mount St. Mary's University	Emmitsburg	MD	1200	26
Mount Saint Mary's University	Los Angeles	CA	1200	26

115

Belhaven University	Jackson	MS	1190	26
Avila University	Kansas City	MO	1190	26
Widener University	Chester	PA	1180	26
University of California at Merced	Merced	CA	1180	26
LaGrange College	LaGrange	GA	1180	26
Clarke University	Dubuque	IA	1170	26
Morehouse College	Atlanta	GA	1170	26
Simpson University	Redding	CA	1170	26
Becker College	Worcester	MA	1170	26
Saint Joseph's College	Rensselaer	IN	1160	26
Mount St. Joseph University	Cincinnati	OH	1160	26
St. Joseph's College -- Brooklyn	Brooklyn	NY	1160	26
McPherson College	McPherson	KS	1160	26
Shenandoah University	Winchester	VA	1160	26
Manchester University	North Manchester	IN	1150	26
Marymount University	Arlington	VA	1150	26
Point Park University	Pittsburgh	PA	1150	26
Aurora University	Aurora	IL	1150	26
Mount Saint Mary College	Newburgh	NY	1150	26
Fresno Pacific University	Fresno	CA	1150	26
Mary Baldwin College	Staunton	VA	1140	26
Lynchburg College	Lynchburg	VA	1140	26
Catawba College	Salisbury	NC	1140	26
Lenoir-Rhyne University	Hickory	NC	1140	26
Huntingdon College	Montgomery	AL	1140	26
Brenau University	Gainesville	GA	1130	26

Wheelock College	Boston	MA	1130	26
Keuka College	Keuka Park	NY	1130	26
Montreat College	Montreat	NC	1130	26
Utica College	Utica	NY	1120	26
Alvernia University	Reading	PA	1120	26
Cazenovia College	Cazenovia	NY	1110	26
University of St. Francis	Joliet	IL	1110	26
Georgian Court University	Lakewood	NJ	1100	26
Sterling College	Sterling	KS	1100	26
Alderson-Broaddus University	Philippi	WV	1100	26
Northwood University - - Michigan Campus	Midland	MI	1100	26
Bethany College	Lindsborg	KS	1090	26
New England College	Henniker	NH	1070	26
St. Xavier University	Chicago	IL	1060	26
Cardinal Stritch University	Milwaukee	WI	1050	26
Bluffton University	Bluffton	OH	1190	25
Texas Lutheran University	Seguin	TX	1170	25
Cedar Crest College	Allentown	PA	1170	25
Wingate University	Wingate	NC	1160	25
University of La Verne	La Verne	CA	1150	25
Menlo College	Atherton	CA	1150	25
Hampton University	Hampton	VA	1150	25
Union College	Barbourville	KY	1140	25
Coastal Carolina University	Conway	SC	1140	25
Marian University Wisconsin	Fond du Lac	WI	1140	25
Lake Erie College	Painesville	OH	1130	25

Missouri Baptist University	St. Louis	MO	1130	25
Caldwell University	Caldwell	NJ	1120	25
Lasell College	Newton	MA	1120	25
Howard Payne University	Brownwood	TX	1120	25
Elms College	Chicopee	MA	1110	25
Bay Path University	Longmeadow	MA	1110	25
Thiel College	Greenville	PA	1110	25
Thomas More College	Crestview Hills	KY	1100	25
Piedmont College	Demorest	GA	1100	25
Long Island University -- C.W. Post Campus	Brookville	NY	1100	25
La Roche College	Pittsburgh	PA	1090	25
Webber International University	Babson Park	FL	1090	25
Grand View University	Des Moines	IA	1090	25
Campbellsville University	Campbellsville	KY	1090	25
Southern Vermont College	Bennington	VT	1070	25
Ferrum College	Ferrum	VA	1050	25
Graceland University	Lamoni	IA	1010	25
Dominican College of Blauvelt	Orangeburg	NY	1010	25
Barclay College	Haviland	KS	1230	24
Rosemont College	Rosemont	PA	1120	24
Mount Mary University	Milwaukee	WI	1100	24
Franklin Pierce University	Rindge	NH	1100	24
Alverno College	Milwaukee	WI	1100	24
Averett University	Danville	VA	1080	24
Our Lady of the Lake University	San Antonio	TX	1080	24

Holy Family University	Philadelphia	PA	1070	24
College of Mount St. Vincent	Riverdale	NY	1060	24
Cabrini College	Radnor	PA	1050	24
Xavier University of Louisiana	New Orleans	LA	1030	24
Bethel University	McKenzie	TN	1160	24
Notre Dame de Namur University	Belmont	CA	1090	23
Curry College	Milton	MA	1090	23
St. Thomas University	Miami Gardens	FL	1090	23
Marymount California University	Rancho Palos Verdes	CA	1060	23
Philander Smith College	Little Rock	AR	1030	23
University of Bridgeport	Bridgeport	CT	1030	23
College of Saint Elizabeth	Morristown	NJ	990	23
Newbury College	Brookline	MA	990	23
Greensboro College	Greensboro	NC	1030	22
Delaware State University	Dover	DE	1020	22
Clark Atlanta University	Atlanta	GA	980	22
Bloomfield College	Bloomfield	NJ	960	22
Dean College	Franklin	MA	1010	21
North Carolina Central University	Durham	NC	1010	21
Felician College	Lodi	NJ	1010	21
Johnson C. Smith University	Charlotte	NC	950	20
Eastern University	St. Davids	PA	1200	20
Juilliard School	New York	NY	n/a	n/a

119

San Francisco Conservatory of Music	San Francisco	CA	n/a	n/a
Ringling College of Art and Design	Sarasota	FL	n/a	n/a
New England Conservatory of Music	Boston	MA	n/a	n/a
New York School of Interior Design	New York	NY	n/a	n/a
Santa Fe University of Art and Design	Santa Fe	NM	n/a	n/a
Campbell University	Buies Creek	NC	n/a	n/a

Chapter 7: How To Politely Ask For More Money So They Can't Say NO

"There are more important things in life than a little money, and one of them is a lot of money."
— Anonymous

Most parents do not realize that you don't have to accept your first offer for financial aid from the colleges. Many colleges will consider an appeal for more financial aid. Colleges call this an appeal process. To do this, you'll need to do write a very detailed and compelling letter asking the financial aid office to consider you for additional funds. The appeal is best used if you have a special circumstance, but sometimes you can also use an award from another school to try to get a better offer. Be careful with this strategy. There is a right way to do this and a wrong way. The overall message of your letter should be that you're requesting enough money so you can make ends meet to have your child to attend the school of his or her first choice school (the school you are appealing to).

While some colleges may respond to competing offers, the absolute best way to get a college to respond to your letter is if you mention special circumstance like the ones listed below:

1. You and/or your parents were employed in 2015 and have been unemployed in 2016.
2. You and/or your parents are receiving less pay in 2016.
3. Since you have applied for financial aid for the 2016-17 academic year, your parents have become separated or divorced.

4. Since you have applied for financial aid for the 2016-17 academic year, one of your parents has died.
5. You and/or your parents had/have medical and dental expenses in 2016 not reimbursed by your insurance.
6. Your parent will pay tuition for private elementary, junior high and/or high school in 2016.
7. You or your parent received unemployment or some untaxed income in 2015 but will no longer receive the benefit in 2016.

Here's an example in a case I did a few years ago where an appeal letter was used:

"Andrew's mother and grandmother came to us with a huge problem. Andrew had been accepted by Dartmouth College, an Ivy League School. Why was this a huge problem? Because the bill was a whopping $54,296 per year! They felt that they had done everything they possibly could to keep the bill down; they had even attended four workshops and hired a firm to turn in their financial aid forms. When I heard their story and met this boy, I was deeply impressed and committed everything I could to the situation; I started looking into ways I could help this family.

I believe in doing your own thorough research rather than assuming that another professional has already asked all of the straightforward questions. After researching the firm and discovering how they submitted the financial aid forms, I realized that Dartmouth was eliminating the family's entire eligibility because the income of three parents had been counted: the two biological parents as well as the stepparent. Another problem was that the already submitted form neglected to mention that the family had an older child in his final year at Kansas State, plus a younger child at a private elementary school in Pasadena.

Our strategy, therefore, was to get the stepparent's income and assets out of the picture, and make Dartmouth aware that the family was also meeting tuition expenses for two other children. I knew that this information could decrease their Expected Family Contribution (EFC) and significantly increase their financial aid eligibility. However, the family's forms, incorrectly filled out, had already been turned in, and there was nothing I could do to change that.

What we could do was write a letter to the financial aid office at Dartmouth, and share the new information and data. As a result, Dartmouth reduced the family's EFC from $55,000 per year to $21,000 per year. This meant that Andrew's yearly financial aid package increased from $5,500 to $37,794. Another way of looking at it was that the family's out-of-pocket costs decreased from $54,296 to $21,958."

Part Two: What You Need To Do To Get The Money

Chapter 8: How To Shop For Colleges That Will Pay You To Attend

"Choose always the way that seems the best, however rough it may be; custom will soon render it easy and agreeable."
— Pythagoras

Once you have your SAT or ACT score out of the way, you need to start looking for colleges to attend. Not all colleges are equal, and they won't all fit your personality and goals. When you're looking for which colleges to apply to, you have to visit them, if possible. It's best to start thinking about this the summer of your sophomore or junior year and visit as many as you can. Visit a large school with over 20,000 undergraduates, visit a medium school with 4-15,000 undergraduates, and visit a small school with 4,000 or less. Visit a school that is in a college town and one that is in an urban area. When you visit, it's best to speak to someone who is a current student that is not part of the admission's team. Ideally you want this person to be at least a sophomore so that they can give you a full perspective. Tell them to be honest with you. Ask what they like so far, what they don't like, what their classes are like, what they're majoring in, and if they have ever changed their major. Ask whatever they think you would like to know. You can ask the admission's department as well, but you can generally get a more objective opinion from a random student.

Take pictures and notes. Trust me, unless you have a photographic memory, you're not going to remember anything more than 10% of what you saw when you visited a college. With pictures and notes you can use them when you're applying to remind yourself about things you'd like to mention in your application. You can inform the admissions board of all the things you like about the school and all the things they brought up as selling points for their university.

Keep in mind when you're walking around that what the school looks like has very little to do with what your experience is going to be, short of needing specific climates for certain activities. I.e., if you surf, you're going to need to be near the ocean. You may find that after about two months you will become accustomed to the school, your routine, and you won't even really notice what the school looks like. It's also important to look at the surrounding area of the school. Most schools look bigger when you first visit them, but once you've lived on campus for a while, you'll realize how small they can become. You may want to find out what there is to do in the town and whether it is a safe area because you will eventually want to live off campus.

One of the most important attributes to keep in mind is the reputation and prestige of the university. It affects what employers think of you, your chances of getting a job, how serious your classmates are, and your graduate school prospects. Although school rankings are a nonstop debate about which version of the rankings is better and whether schools should be ranked at all, there is a relationship between how high your school is ranked and your school's national and regional academic reputation. The most prominent college ranking list is the US News and Princeton Review. These are third party sources that evaluate colleges based on their mission, financial aid packages, cost, attrition rates, majors, lifestyle, and a slew of other factors. To understand this more you can search for Princeton Review college rankings and US News Report College Rankings Evaluation.

Remember, rankings should be taken with a grain of salt because once a school is ranked in the top 400, there are very few differences in the resources you or your student will have. Any differences in the student's success will come down to the resources they actually use and how well they do academically and socially at that school. We look at rankings as one factor, but finding a school that's right for your family is more important.

Before we begin to narrow down our college search, you must take a second to evaluate how good each school is for financial aid and who they tend to charge money. It's also important to understand what a college will offer you as your net price, out-of-pocket cost. Go to the school's website and see if they offer any information about the school's net price. Some schools will just list their prices while others will offer a net price calculator that can give you a ballpark figure of what your out-of-pocket costs will be. If the number scares you, don't worry. There is a lot of help available for students and their parents.

Once you know the net price, you need to look at how large the student body, departments, and classrooms are. These factors can tell you how much attention you will get in the classroom and how much access you will actually have to the professor who teaches the classes. It also affects who will be offering help during office hours: the professor or a graduate student. You can look at the student-to-faculty ratio to get an idea of this. While many large schools provide great resources academically, it is important to see if the school's resources are appropriate for your needs. The knowledge and skills you will walk away with and the people you interact with will all determine the quality of your network.

When you're looking at a school, take a second to think about what kind of lifestyle change you'll need to make. How often will you see your family? How close is it to your friends? What activities can you participate in that you will be able to continue doing at the school, whether through classes, gym access, or in the local community? How quickly and often can you get family support?

There's definitely a benefit to attending a college close to where you live because at any time you can come home when you're tired of the dorm food or want to see a familiar face. Some of the colleges that you will be attending will have more students from that state than anything else. You'll find that on three day weekends, or on any given weekend, many of the students will go home and the college becomes a ghost town. If you are from out of state, that aspect could be a downside for you if you want people to interact with. You'd be one of the few students that are left at the school while everyone else is at home. When I was young, I wanted to get as far away from home as possible and experience being independent, but I also found out how much I really value being with my family.

You'll also find that if you go to a school in another state but you intend to start your career in your home town, most of your contacts and network are in the state where you attend college. This is especially true if your home town is smaller and many people do not leave the area. Your first internship may be in another state, or your degree might be more accepted in one part of the United States rather than another. Keep in mind that if you get your degree in Chemical Engineering, there are not a lot of opportunities for people with your skills in small town USA, so you'll likely have to relocate to an area that has a demand for what you studied. You must take this into consideration when you are picking colleges.

There is no doubt that if you are trying to find a college that will provide you with scholarships, you will find one but don't limit yourself to only a few. You must realize that the more schools you are willing to look at, the more opportunities you have to receive money. It is still important to consider what kinds of lifestyle changes you will need to make in order to get this education so you also don't just choose the first school that offers you a decent financial aid package. Keep in mind the following questions when looking at the different schools to get a better understanding of whether you will fit in that school.

How good is the school for your major? What do most people study at this school?: Some schools are great overall, but when it comes to a particular major, you might find that very few students major in that topic. This is important because a university will more than likely commit their funds to their most successful programs. Likewise, you might find that a college is more or less unknown nationally, but they are one of the top schools that specialize in one particular kind of major. They can have a lot of money dedicated to that department, which means more resources and opportunities. Finding a school that is great for a specific major can be very challenging; the best place to start is by doing Internet research and then comparing the programs to one another. Also remember that each college has a particular program of which they take great pride. For each college you visit, ask the admissions department as well as the student body, what those programs are.

How many majors are offered?: Along with knowing whether a college offers your major, it is equally important to understand how many other majors the college offers in case you change your major, double major, or want a minor. If you have even the slightest inclination that you might change your major, it is better to pick the university that offers many majors so that you are not stuck at a school that is only good for a specific major.

What new life experiences will you encounter?: In four years a lot can happen. If you're looking for a different life experience, like being in a different part of the country or world, it's important to see what kind of life experiences you will have. Remember that you are there to get an education first and foremost, but if you want to know what it's like to live in the big city, then you can consider a college that will offer a very different way of life than the one you have now.

What else is there to do in that town?: As mentioned before, after the first two to three months, the college will seem a lot smaller than you remembered, and the town will become more and more important. When you are not studying or on the campus, you may want to do other things. If there are things that you like to do and hobbies that you like, you will want to consider whether this campus and town can offer you chances to participate in them.

What are the people like?: The people at a college are very important. You must feel like the people that attend the school are like you. It lends itself to how many friends you will have, because you will already have things in common. You will have a good idea of what your social experience will be like in college. You don't need to seek out homogeny, but you should consider how much of the student body shares your mindset, values your life experiences, and how much you have in common with the student body. It's easier to create a community feel if you already have something in common.

How big is the school?: Many students say that they want to attend a big school. They may have attended high schools that were very small. If you like meeting new people, it may be appealing to attend a big school, but you must understand that it is unlikely that the entire student body will be your friend. After you've graduated, you'll notice that most of the people you still speak to are more than likely a core group of friends that you have things in common with. Also, a large school can often be isolating and impersonal. The best way to describe it is to compare a city like New York City to a really small town in Middle America. Even though there are more people in New York, it does not mean that you will know more people. Be aware that the bigger the city, the less people see it as a point of commonality. I'm not dissuading you from picking a big school by the way. I went to a fairly large school, but you don't want to discount a school just because it is a not considered large. There are many advantages to going to a smaller school such as class sizes and a stronger sense of community.

How active is the student body?: There are definitely schools where students take pride in the educational institution they represent. There are colleges where students really do a great job of adding to the college experience and raising their opinions about the activities the school offers and things they want to change. On the other hand, there are universities where everyone is just focused on getting their degree. Neither one is better than the other; they are just different.

Is the school liberal or conservative?: If you have a certain political ideology or set of beliefs that you hold dear, you'll want to do the research to see how much of the college agrees with your ideology. You'll also find that the ideology of the school has much to do with what part of the United States the school is located. Let's say you are very "left wing" and you go to a school that is very conservative. You might find that you do not agree with the average student's viewpoint on a particular topic. Or you may find that the speakers the school brings in or who they choose to honor do not resonate well with you.

What's the school's religious affiliation?: More than half of the private colleges in America have some type of religious affiliation. I'd say that the most obvious way to tell how religiously affiliated a school is to look at the essay questions they ask. Most will ask you point blank what your viewpoint is of their doctrine. It can make the difference in acceptance as well. If you are of a particular religion or went to a high school that shares the same religious beliefs as your prospective college, you'll find

133

that the colleges will like that you already share their values. Don't discount schools based on religion, however. The degree to which religion is included as a part of the campus experience will vary greatly. When I was looking for colleges, I made it a point to avoid colleges that provided any religious direction as a part of their curriculum, but I regretted it later. When you go to college, much of what you will be learning is the information to help you to figure out who you are and how you want to live your life. Although you may not want to follow every doctrine presented to you, you will want to understand what other religions believe. Also, just understand that if you are going to attend a private school, the chances of your college having some type of religious affiliation is high, so it helps to look at how the college approaches religion before you write it off completely.

What's the culture of the student body (party, study, school spirit)?: Much like how active the student body is in school issues, it is also important to get a general idea from current students as to what most people in the school are there to do. It's a sweeping generalization, and the answer will likely vary by department or college within a university. However, you'll want to know if you are going to a school where most people are there to prepare for graduate school, party, watch their sports team, or simply use it as a post high school daycare. You'll also want to see how many of the students live on campus versus commute because this will affect how many people you interact with on a daily basis.

Where do you stand as a student? (How much of a challenge is this going to be for you?): You'll want to know if you would be considered academically above average, average, or below average. I don't think there is anything wrong with being a below average student. In fact, it can be impressive because you were accepted out of many other students that may have had stronger credentials.

However, when it comes to the classroom, where you stand academically will definitely determine your GPA at the school. Most of my students say that college is much harder than high school and whatever GPA you have in high school, you can assume it will be half a point to a full point lower in college (unless you've mastered the study topics mentioned in this book). If you are planning to attend graduate school, consider a college where you will get a good GPA.

Is the school co-ed or all-girls or boys?: Many students will also write off a college if it is not co-ed without knowing what is around the college, i.e., a brother or sister college. There are many all-girls and all-boys schools located right next to their counterpart colleges so the students can still interact. In fact, many of these colleges allow students of the opposite sex to attend classes at their brother or sister school. It's best to ask the college how well they are at integrating the college experience with neighboring colleges.

How powerful is the alumni network?: You want to know if you call alumni, if they will feel any kind of affinity towards you. This is important because when you start your career, perhaps your best network to draw from will be from your college. You'll want to know if the alums will be willing to help you because you also will participate in their program. It's not a perfect measure but you can ask what percent of alumni donate to the college. The answer to this question will give you an idea of how much people care about their school and the upcoming students, especially after they've graduated.

How are the sports teams?: First of all, let me reiterate that you are going to college to get an education. Even if you are there to play a sport, your education is the number one priority. You are a student first before you are an athlete. With that said, if you love a particular sport and you want to continue playing it during college, a good sports team is a great reason to pick a school.

Understand where your school fits academically for your major before you select it for the sport. Do not simply plan to attend a college just for their basketball team. Many of those colleges are great for basketball, but not for anything else. Plus, there is no guarantee that you will "go pro." I'm all for aiming toward the stars, but the statistics show that 75% of students who play a sport their freshmen year, leave the team by their senior year. The stats are even lower for athletes who "go pro." At some point in your life, you will need to figure out who you are outside of that sport. It may be after 20 years of playing the game or it may be after one year in college. However, the longer you put that conversation off, the more likely you are to put yourself in a situation where you do not have any other skills other than your athletic ability. You could get injured during your first game, or even the pre-season, and never play that sport in college or as a professional again. Enjoy the game and let it open doors for you, but remember that at the end of the day, it's your education that will follow you and open the doors for you long term.

How safe is the campus?: You'll need to understand how safe your college campus is and much of this has to do with the surrounding area of your college. Review the measures your college has taken to make sure that the students are safe to walk around the campus. This can include courtesy numbers that you can call for escorts, gates around the campus, or having the people check ID cards before entering different buildings, like the dorms. You want to ask these questions to the admissions office and the students.

Does the school have a campus feel?: Some campuses are very well-gated, and it takes a bit of effort to arrive on campus. Some colleges are part of the city. Take NYU and Boston University, for instance. These campuses consist of buildings throughout the city that belong to the university. On the other hand there are colleges where the entire city or town belongs to the college. Each type of campus has a different feel. This can include things like having a place where you can lie on the lawn and study or having to travel by bus to get to your class in another building that's across town.

What unique activities does the school offer?: Some schools have many different clubs, programs or organizations that are affiliated with the school. If the school offers an activity that resonates with you, like movie clubs, religious youth groups, or an investor club, this can be a great reason to pick a school.

How are the facilities and living conditions?: You want to know what your living situation will look like when you attend the college. How large are the dorms and how many students are placed in each room? Where are the dining halls and is there a fitness center? How many libraries are there and how close are they to the dorms? How easy or difficult is it to get Wi-Fi? These are all questions that you need to ask before you decide where to attend.

Does the school have a strong career office?: This is another very important factor. You want to know how much the college has invested in taking care of their students when they graduate. It's great to get a degree, but if you can't find a job and have no support in your job search, it can be very frustrating. For many students, they are going to college in order to get a good first job to use as a stepping stone in their career. Is there a particular industry or profession that you would like to explore? Find out how many students got into that field right out of college. The career center should be able to help you. How much you get out of the career center will relate to how much you utilize it. However, be aware that some colleges will have much more involved and sophisticated career offices than others.

How is the Greek life?: Some schools are a great for Greek life; some schools are anti-Greek altogether. If you're planning to join a sorority or fraternity, or if the idea appeals to you, you will want to know what percentage of students are in those organizations at the college and whether there is Greek housing. Also you will want to consider how much of your college experience you will want to dedicate to Greek life.

Chapter 9: How To Choose The Best Major & Career To Make You Shine

"I have found the best way to give advice to your children is to find out what they want and then advise them to do it."
— Harry S. Truman

In order to narrow down your major you must know what skills you have and understand what careers are available that could be a fit for you. You must have an open mind and be willing to try things until you find something that works for you.

Personality Assessments like MBTI (Myers-Briggs Type Indicator)

The Myers-Briggs Type Indicator is a test used to measure someone's social and decision-making preferences and inclinations. In other words, these tests can help to figure out what things you prefer to do and skills you have. For instance, they can suggest if you are better at working with people, working individually, or if you are quantitatively (mathematically) inclined versus qualitatively (analytically) inclined. The results of your exam will recommend a certain career area that is your best fit. It doesn't mean that you have to stop doing well in things that are not necessarily your strengths. And you don't have to study something that matches your ideal preferences. I studied accounting, and my personality type is almost the complete opposite of what makes for a good accountant. You can become excellent at any skills that you want if you are determined. Just keep in mind that if you are doing something that is not your preference, it will be a little more difficult to master than for someone who is naturally inclined. Simply use these assessments for suggestions.

Skills for Career Building

Create a bucket list of the things that you want to accomplish in your life and work backward to see what skills you will need to accomplish your bucket list. I knew that I wanted to be a business owner and that accounting was a good skill set to have to keep good track of my business and investments. For example, if you want to work in Washington, D.C. as someone lobbying for their needs and interests, it's good to have a background in business and political science to understand the political and commercial landscape.

Market Need

If you complete a personality assessment exam online, you can find majors that correspond to the personality type. However, you must pay attention to the projected demand for people in the field recommended. If you are interested in something that has a very small market for that kind of skill and knowledge, consider combining it with other fields to become more marketable. If you have strong skills in English but you find that there is little demand for an English major, you could consider Communications, Journalism, Advertising and Screenwriting. These majors apply your knowledge of English to a particular industry. However, keep in mind, and accept that your major may change at least once in college because you may start taking classes and realize you really don't like the subject as much as you thought or prefer another. Keep trying new things until something works for you. Talk to people that do the job and make sure to do internships so you can get practical knowledge of the field. It will help you choose a good major and career path for yourself.

Chapter 10: Qualifying For College Is Easier Than You Think

*"Education is not a preparation for life;
education is life itself."*
— John Dewey

Before you get too gung ho about any particular college, spend some time making sure you are the kind of student they are looking for. Have you met all of their academic requirements? Look over their admission's page to see if you have taken the necessary coursework. Have you seen the profile of an average student who was admitted? You can get that information by talking to your counselor, doing some Internet research or visiting the school. Make sure you are looking at an average student who's been admitted for unique reasons. It is best when you can actually meet a student or recent graduate who was admitted to the college that you are interested in attending so that you can see what you need to do and say to be accepted. There is no guarantee that just because you have similar attributes to someone who was already admitted that you will be admitted as well. However, this gives you a model to go after and helps you to set the standard for what information you need to showcase to the admissions board. Take a look at what they brought to the table, but be yourself.

SAT/ACT Scores

I would say that the best and easiest indicator of whether you qualify for a college is the average SAT or ACT scores of the students who were admitted last year. What are the bottom 25% and the top 75% of the scores? This will give you a really good range of the scores you need to achieve to be considered the kind of student that a college tends to admit. These stats should obviously not be the sole determinant. In fact, the more competitive the school the less interested they are in near perfect SAT or ACT scores, furthermore there are many successfully admitted students whose SAT or ACT scores are their worst attributes. The truth in most cases is that you can pretty quickly size up someone's chances of getting into a college and receiving a scholarship just by comparing their SAT or ACT scores to the average student at the college, unless there's something remarkable about the candidate or he or she has a rare minority status. If I looked at the average SAT scores for the colleges that I applied to and made that the "be all end all" reason for whether or not I should apply, I wouldn't have the degree I have now from BU. However, it is important to know what your chances are, so that you're not kidding yourself or setting yourself up for a mailbox full of rejection letters.

Average GPA

Some schools do not require SAT or ACT scores so you should also look at the average weighted and unweighted GPA of the students that have been admitted to a particular college. This information can be searched online or on Collegeboard.org. Weighted GPA can be above 4.0 to taken into account more difficult courses like community college, AP, IB and honors classes. Unweighted GPA will simply tell you what the average grade the student has gotten without looking at how hard the class was. When you research a college you might see that most people have a gap of 3.5 to 3.75 unweighted GPA. This is very helpful so that you can see where you stand in relation to the college. Another good way to find out if your GPA is competitive at a particular school is to ask your counselor to tell or show you the GPA of a student who was admitted to a particular college from your high school. Maybe a student was accepted last year or a few years ago. Of course, this doesn't tell you the whole story, but it can give you some benchmarks and perhaps some minimum requirements.

Availability Of Your Major

Departments and universities are not always equal. There will be some majors that are harder to get into depending on what university you apply to. For instance, if you want to major in business, University of Pennsylvania, Massachusetts Institute of Technology, or University of California, Berkeley are likely to set the standard and as a result, will have more rigorous admissions requirements. Even if you don't think that you can get into those top schools you should still be looking at what makes them so great so you have a benchmark when you are looking at other schools.

Acceptance Rate

Acceptance rates are an important figure but should be taken with a grain of salt. It does not necessarily determine how selective the school is or how prestigious they are; it has more to do with how many seats the school has available and how many students apply each year. There are many schools that receive more applications than a prestigious university because that school is just more well-known for something, like sports, for instance. Acceptance rates are important to look at when you are looking at highly selective colleges because many of these colleges just do not have the room for all the students that are qualified. You'll see acceptance rates as low as 6% (or less), meaning that one in every 16 to 17 people gets accepted. You can be sure that of those 16-17 competing applicants that do not get accepted, many of them were still very qualified.

Other Things To Mildly Consider

Alumni relation: If you are closely related to an alum or are the descendant of a very influential alum, this can help. For instance, if your sister also went to the school, or your great grandfather donated, this helps, but it won't guarantee admission. You must still demonstrate that you would not flunk out of the program if you were given an opportunity.

Geographic residence: Some schools want to have students from very small or underrepresented parts of the United States like small towns or from different socioeconomic statuses in order to increase the diversity of the classroom. They do this to improve the experience that you have with your classmates. If you are coming from an underrepresented group or even state, you may find it a little easier to be admitted, but once again, this is assuming that you are already academically qualified. Remember that the competitions for getting into college are so high that you can be rejected even though you are qualified.

Religion: If you represent an underrepresented religion or your declared religion is the same as that of the school, you can also expect a little bit of leniency from the colleges in terms of acceptance. Many schools want to make sure that students are academically qualified, and that they will carry on their faith and participate in their religious activities with enthusiasm. It is smart to pick a school of the same religion as your church or your high school if it is religious. You can also consider a recommendation from someone who knows you from some capacity of worship if the schools haven't already asked.

State residency: If you live near the school. The schools can also tend to accept you for being a local student. For instance if you are from Eagle Rock, you may have a better chance of getting accepted to Occidental College or if you are from Harlem, you can have a better shot of getting accepted to Columbia all things being equal.

Chapter 11: 4-Deadlines You Don't Want To Miss

"When you do nothing, you feel overwhelmed and powerless. But when you get involved, you feel the sense of hope and accomplishment that comes from knowing you are working to make things better."
— Albert Einstein

College	Submission Period
Most State Universities	October 1st - December 1st
University of California	November 1st – November 30th
California State Universities:	October 1st - November 30th
Private Colleges:	October 1st - February 1st
Financial Aid:	October 1st - March 1st

Check with each college individually to find out their due dates. Be aware that most state colleges have earlier deadlines than private universities.

You need to know how much time you actually have to put an application together. I really recommend no less than two months to get an application ready and that is assuming you're starting from scratch. I.e., you don't have your main personal statement and other application materials ready to go. Some schools will grant you an extension if you are past the deadline, but don't count on it. If you're late, you must put together a spectacular application and already look like the kind of student the school would accept.

To get a general idea about deadlines—as in, what month a school usually requires you to submit your application—you must take the information directly from the school's website as that will be the most up-to-date information.

There are three major types of application deadlines: early decision, early action, and regular decision. You can find these deadlines on the school's admissions page. Approximately 450 colleges have early decision or early action plans, and some have both. Some colleges offer a nonbinding option called single-choice, early action under which applicants can only apply for one college under that plan. Applications for other colleges will have to be Regular Decision.

Early Decision

Early Decision is a binding contract between the family and university. It stipulates that if a university accepts the student, they must attend the university. These applications are usually due first. Early Decision has come under fire as unfair to low income students since they do not have the opportunity to compare financial aid offers.

Early Action

Early Action is non-binding. It is simply an opportunity to turn your application in earlier to get your decision faster. These applications are also due before the Regular Decision deadline. Early Action is good. Do Early Action.

Regular Decision

The regular decision deadline is simply when most of the applications are due. There is no major downside to turning in your application at the regular decision deadline, especially if it gives you more time to put together a better application.

Chapter 12: The Most Important Parts Of The Application & Overview

"The man who is prepared has his battle half fought."
— Miguel De Cervantes

Everything has brought you to this point. You've researched the different schools, narrowed down your major, determined if you qualify, and looked at the scholarship opportunities available. It's now time to apply. You should have a working list of schools that you are evaluating based on your criteria. You know which ones will be better for you than others. You want to narrow down this list to 10. It's okay to change the list later, but in order to move onto the next phase you have to narrow them down. Once you've decided on what 10 schools to apply to, find out when the applications are due and what these schools require in order to submit an application.

As you look at colleges, you'll find that a few of them will take the same application or that several of them use different ones. You need to know which applications your colleges accept because it will help you know what essay questions they will ask and how long it can take to complete their application. There are three major categories of college application types, state school applications, the Common Application, and non-Common App private school applications. Even though there are different types of applications they will all ask for similar information.

1. **State School Applications:** Applications that you can use to apply to certain schools in a state like ApplyTexas, which allows you to apply to any Texas public university, UC Admissions, which allows you to apply to any University of

California, or CSU Mentor, which allows you to apply to Cal States.
2. **Common Application:** An application that works for over 500 different universities in 47 different states and the District of Columbia.
3. **Non-Common App Private School Applications:** Some private schools like Georgetown, MIT, Rose-Holman, and Azusa Pacific University, have their very own application.

Components of Most Applications

School Report/Transcripts: This part of the application is completed by your counselors. Your counselor sends the schools your grades, gives a short evaluation of any disciplinary action that you have experienced, and gives a broad recommendation to the college.

Activities Form: This is the part of the applicant where you list every activity, both volunteer and work experience you have been significantly involved in since the 9th grade. Take a look at the activities form at the first opportunity by creating a login, so that you can see what you will need to include when it's your turn to apply. The key here is to sit with your parents and anyone else that really has watched you grow throughout high school and have them tell you the things they remember that they thought were impressive.

Midyear Report: Some schools will ask for a midyear report which is the grades for the first semester of your senior year. It's important to not slack off your senior year of high school.

Final Report: Once your senior year has been completed, some schools will ask for a final report.

Teacher Evaluations: Many colleges will require recommendation letters from a teacher. Though it may vary based on the application, most schools are asking the teacher to evaluate you on a scale of one to seven based on the characteristics below:

a. Academic achievement
b. Intellectual promise
c. Quality of writing
d. Creative, original thought
e. Productive class discussion
f. Respect accorded to the faculty
g. Disciplined work habits
h. Maturity
i. Motivation
j. Leadership
k. Integrity
l. Reaction to setbacks
m. Concern for others
n. Self-confidence
o. Initiative
p. Independence

Keep all this in mind because when we review essays, these attributes will also become important.

Counselor and/or other evaluations: Along with evaluations from your teacher, many schools will require the same evaluation from your counselor, pastors, or peers.

Interview: The more competitive or small the school is, the more likely there is to be a mandatory interview the college will hold to bring a face to the application.

Essays: Lastly, there is the essay. Although the essay is the last point, it is the most important part of a college application because it allows you the most room for creativity in the application.

Chapter 13: How To Send Your Transcript & SAT Scores

"Success is the sum of details."
— Harvey S. Firestone

Go to your counselor or registrar and have them send your official transcript to each college or scholarship you are considering. If you have taken classes at any community college or through summer programs that provide high school credit, be sure to send those transcripts as well. Send your SAT scores from College Board and your ACT scores from ACT.org. If you know what colleges you are going to apply to and their university code, when you are registering, you can include this information, and your scores will automatically be sent when they are calculated. It is a good idea to ask a college what is the last SAT/ACT test date they will accept scores from if you need to retake an exam.

Chapter 14: Extracurricular Activities, Work & Volunteering That Make You Look Special

"I was raised to volunteer: nursing homes, clinics, church nurseries, and schools, everywhere that could use help. It's such an intrinsic part of me, to use my life to help improve the quality of others."
— Debby Ryan

When it comes to picking extracurricular activities to focus on throughout your high school career and which ones you are going to put on your application, it is important that you don't try to do what everybody else is doing. Be different. If everybody is in Key Club or is part of the National Society for High School Scholars, you won't stand out when you apply. Unless you have a strong passion for that topic and are willing to put more time and energy into it than anybody else at your school—and in some instances, more time than the other students across the nation—it's best that you just be yourself and pick one or two activities to do well. These activities do not have to be offered at your high school. There are plenty of interests you can have outside of high school and when it's time to stand out, you want to sound different than all the other class presidents that are applying.

High school sports, traveling sports, academic decathlons, film competitions, art competitions, shows and performances are all events that you can join and compete in. Sometimes winning or placing in a competition can do more for you than being in any club in high school. If you have a very interesting hobby that you take very seriously, make sure you don't leave it out of your application. Creativity is a big thing that colleges look for. Part of what they are trying to do is get a good mix of creators and innovators to attend their schools. If you started an eBay business or were a DJ, a choreographer, or break dancer, etc. make sure you mention it.

On the other hand, you can decide to attend a summer program. There are many summer programs for high school students that are usually held on university campuses. They can range from one to seven weeks long and provide you with an experience of what it is like to be in college. You will be living in the dorms with other high school students and if the program is very good, they will also teach academic classes that can be used for high school/AP credit. I find that these programs attract some of the most competitive students in the nation. I went to a similar program at Georgetown University and I met about five students that ended up at Harvard the following year. After going through this program, I finally saw who I was really competing against.

If you do go the typical high school club route, make sure that your contributions are measurable, interesting, and demonstrate leadership. Your high school will have clubs that are exclusive to your school, and some will be chapters of national or regional organizations. You can also form your own club. The name of the game here is not to be club president, vice president, or treasurer for the title. If you were president of your club but under your leadership the club did nothing differently, in fact declined in membership, this experience is not going to have much value. When people ask you about your days in the club they want to hear actual accomplishments. If you increased membership, raised a large amount of funds, or provided a long needed retreat or cultural experience for your team, these are measurable and should be noted in your application.

Sometimes you have to work and you have no time to volunteer or do extracurricular activities; that's good, too. If you had to work in a body shop or help your parents with their business, such activity shows that you are determined, and you can manage multiple responsibilities. Be sure to mention what you do on the job, especially if you trained people, were complimented on something you did, or if there is something on the job that only you are trusted to do.

Lastly, don't underestimate what experiences would be worth talking about especially if you have ever lived, stayed, or visited another country. Think about missions you have been on or family trips. An example of this would be those who spend their summers in Nicaragua with their church. If you don't think these experiences would be good in the activities section of the application, they usually can make for a very good essay. Be sure to take a day or two to sit down and think about all the places you have been and things you have done.

This is not the time to be a mysterious person. You have to present the college with every single reason why they need to accept you. Don't think that just because your extracurricular activity isn't academic, like decathlons, or traditional, like piano, that it's not credible. Do things that interest you, not what you think will interest an admission officer. When in doubt, run it by someone. If it is interesting and measureable, include it in your application.

Chapter 15: How To Get Powerful Evaluations & Valuable Recommendation Letters

"Personality can open doors,
but only character can keep them open."
— Elmer G. Leterman

We covered this before, but you will end up needing recommendations from your teachers, counselor, and possibly your pastor if your school has a strong religious affiliation. Pick teachers that have strong academic credibility and teach academic classes. Don't pick the teachers that let you slack off or haven't been teaching for a long period of time unless they are extraordinarily passionate about their subject. Think about what teachers you have the best relationship with and who can speak of your academic ability. It helps if you were the kind of student who met with the teacher to go over the class objectives and sat in the front. Consider teachers that have seen you demonstrate strong effort and improvement. For instance, if you struggled in a class, and then you started to rise to the occasion, this teacher is a great person to ask for a recommendation letter. Don't be afraid to ask. You'd be surprised at how many teachers you considered mean would jump at the opportunity to write you a recommendation letter. Some teachers are hard on you because they know you will make it to college, and they want to toughen you up so you won't be surprised when you finally get there.

A good evaluation letter with good writing can be very persuasive. Find someone who could actually *write* a good recommendation. The teacher should have information about you, and he or she should try to demonstrate a positive vision to the college. If the teacher is not good at convincing anyone of a point of view, he or she may not make a good reference. This is tricky because most of the time you will not be able to see what they write, so you have to think about this when you choose who to ask. When I pick people to write references and recommendations for me, I pick people that I know are going to convince others to take their recommendations seriously.

Give the evaluator a brag sheet. Don't assume your teachers know your whole life story or any of your other talents if you have not repeatedly demonstrated them. Write up a list of the activities, projects you have completed, and your career goals and give it to them so that they have some content to reference when they write your letter. Tell them how you're trying to present yourself. The teacher or counselor is obviously supposed to write what they think of you, but you want to give them an idea of how you want them to present you. If you have written your essays already, you can show them drafts so that they don't share the same information in their letter. You want the admissions board to get a well-rounded image of you.

Make sure that your recommender actually knows you. Yes, you want to give your recommender content to work with, but this person is still supposed to be able to share new and unique information about you. In any recommendation letter, one of the first questions a recommender must be able to answer is how long they have known you and in what capacity. An endorsement from someone who doesn't know you well has little credibility even if it comes from an otherwise highly influential person. A glowing recommendation from your AP English teacher is better than a generic letter from the mayor. When you don't have a good grade in a class, or you have a grade that sticks out like a sore thumb, I highly suggest getting a recommendation from the teacher that gave you the worst or one of your worst grades. They may have at least a few good things to say about you and can explain what happened in that class. Their explanation is often much more credible than yours. So if you earned a "D" in a class, a letter from that teacher would be helpful if there is a good explanation for the grade; i.e., you were battling a disease during that school year.

Sometimes you get extra room on an application to write additional information that should be considered. Always use this opportunity to explain a bad grade or anything else that sticks out poorly in your application. Never leave a college to make its own conclusion about something questionable. EVER!

Chapter 16: What Makes You Different Than Everybody Else?

"Common sense is genius dressed in its working clothes."
— Ralph Waldo Emerson

Before we can get to the essay portion of the application, you have to know what makes you unique. For some people, it's best to almost look at themselves as fictional characters with certain traits, because it's not always easy to answer the question: what makes you unique? People are generally their worst critics; however, the essay is the one place where you can show off your talents and really talk to the admissions board. It can make you stand out. The best way to know what you have to offer is to list all your characteristics by clustering.

The questions to ask yourself follow:

What's interesting about me? What are the things that most people would not know about me? What combination of characteristics, stories and details would allow people to quickly see what I would be like in real life? Some of the best applications/essays include two things about a person that you wouldn't foresee, i.e., being a skateboarder who is also interested in science. That combination is interesting to the admissions board. Take time and brainstorm. Get as many traits or stories about yourself on paper so you have this in your arsenal when it's time to write your essays.

Your circle of influence will say a lot about who you are or at least allow the college application essay reader to imagine what you would be like. The way that most people get to know you is not by your credentials and accomplishments but by getting to know you as a human being. Think about a presidential candidate. You might find that although some people are influenced by the candidates' "badges," most are influenced by how they live their lives and who they are as a human beings. There are a lot of traits, people, and places that impact who you are and how you live your life. Some things to think about are:

Family: How would you describe your parents? What do you admire about them? What impact have they made on your life? Is your family small or is it large? What do you all have in common? It is almost guaranteed that a school will ask you about your life; they are expecting to hear something about your family.

Your high school: What is your school like? Is it homogenous, diverse, academic, competitive, or close-knit? What your current school is like may have an influence on what you are looking for in a university. It can also impact how well you fit within the student body at the university.

Neighborhood: What's your neighborhood like? Is it urban, suburban, rural, conservative, liberal, affluent, or impoverished? How do the people live their lives, and is it a close knit community? What is the town known for?

Friends: What are your friends like and what is your relationship with them like? Are you the voice of reason or excitement? Are you the ringleader or the implementer?

Mentors: Who has made a significant impact in your life besides your parents? What have you learned from them?

Books you've read: What books have you read that really changed your world view or that you would suggest to someone else? Why?

What is a credible source of information: Where do you get your information from? Where do you get your news?

Religion: What's your religion? How has this influenced you, if at all?

How would most people describe you to a college: Ask your family and friends to describe you in five words. You'll learn a lot about what makes you different.

Travel: I've lived in a few places in my life like New York, Boston, Dallas, Los Angeles, and Belize. I've also lived in different places within those cities and countries. Was this you or did you grow up in the same place all your life? How does that make you unique?

Earliest childhood memory: What do you remember about your childhood that describes how you grew up a little differently?

What don't people know about you?: Is there anything that you tend to keep secret from people like a special talent or unique experience? As I've said before, the application is not a place to be shy. Ask your parents and grandparents this question as well. They are likely to have some funny, cute or embarrassing story about you.

Favorite quote: Is there a quote that describes your ideology? The easier you can find something that defines who you are at your core, the easier it is to paint a picture to the admissions board about who you are. It makes it easier to remember you.

Dreams: What are your dreams? What would you want to come true? What are you working toward and why are you working towards it?

Quirks: While listing these, be careful when putting any of these in your essays. Run this by someone before you submit the application, but if there is something a little weird about you that people find a little annoying, but funny, you might be able to use it. For instance when I was little I used to eat peanut butter and ketchup sandwiches. Don't judge. It's definitely weird, but I bet you'll remember this about me above everything.

Random things you like: If you're an eclectic person and you like things that most people wouldn't think you'd like, make note of them. It's golden.

Idea or invention you thought of: If you've ever thought of a solution to a common problem, feasible or not, take note of the idea.

What you strongly believe in: There may be a cause, like autism or preserving the environment, which you strongly believe in. This is always good to add because it allows people to understand your values.

Worldview: If you could sum up your view of the world in one concrete philosophy, this is very powerful. For instance, "you cause everything that happens to you in your life," shows that you are willing to take responsibility for who you are and where you are in life.

When did you decide you wanted to go to college: You'll want to have handy a concrete set of reasons for why you are going to college and what you expect to get out of your college experience. A good five to seven reasons is great.

Your bucket list: A list of all things you would like to accomplish in life shows that you have a vision. Once I wrote a eulogy of myself in a college essay. It was a story about me when I died at 45 and all the things people said as a tribute to me. It gave the reader an understanding of my life goals in a unique way.

What does paradise and utopia look like to you: What does the perfect world look like to you? Obviously this doesn't have to be feasible, but it would give us a strong sense of your values.

Something you tried whether you succeeded or failed: This topic digs deep into life experiences. Think of any life experiences that you would consider defining moments. Any moments that speak to your characteristics or moments that you can really reflect on are good to document.

Characteristics you admire in other people: If we can understand what characteristics you admire in other people, we can see that what you value. This says a lot about you and the future you. Characteristics that you value can be honesty, love, compassion, respect, and honor.

Injuries: Injuries and near death experiences that you've had or witnessed can make for good stories, especially if they show how you overcame them.

There is a lot more to this and I could go on and on. Do as much of this as you can. Not only will it be a lot easier for you to answer the essay and interview questions, it will teach you a lot about yourself and help you to grasp your identity.

Chapter 17: How To Master A College Essay

"Character development is the great,
if not the sole, aim of education."
— William O'Shea

Now, it's time to write the essay. When I'm working with a student, I often spend the most time helping them with this section of the application. I guarantee that you will too if you really are dedicated to the pursuit of enrollment and acceptance into a good college. Follow the tips in this chapter, and you'll be well on your way to a great first draft essay. The first few things that you need to know are to start early, ponder the essay topics well, and gather all your background information first.

Start early. Masterpiece essays take time. About 30% of that time is spent completing prewriting exercises and another 50% considering the prompt. The rest is spent on the editing process, so make sure you have given yourself ample time before the deadline to complete it.

Consider the topics. I don't recommend that you write an answer to the essay prompt the moment you read it. Look at the prompts for every school you are applying to, think about how you're going to answer each of them, and notice which questions are very similar. Try a few different methods of answering the prompt and then outline how you're going to approach each essay before you even write your first draft. Give yourself at least a week just to think about the prompt.

Gather all your background information first. Get your ideas all out on one sheet of paper. If you haven't already done so, go back to the previous chapter and make a cluster of what makes you unique. Spend at least 30 minutes to an hour on this. When you first start writing, you'll note your most obvious character traits, but as you keep making new clusters you will start to discover really unique traits about yourself that are less likely to be considered trite in an essay. As a rule of thumb, if it took you 60 seconds to come up with an idea, chances are it took someone else the same 60 seconds. It is apparent when it takes only a few minutes for someone to come up with an answer.

Once you have all your thoughts figured out, you can start writing your first draft. Here is an example of a main essay prompt: *"Describe the world you come from."* You might see different versions of this question from different schools, but on some level you can argue that most college essays are simply asking you the above prompt. Look through all the essay prompts from all the schools you are considering and work on answering the most common prompt. You want to put time into this prompt first for two reasons. First, most colleges will ask this question, so if you really work on the creation of a solid answer, such will give them context to understand your entire application. Second, it helps you understand your main message and creates a skeleton for your application.

Subsequent to sharing the description of your life with the admissions board, the second most asked essay question is, *"Why XYZ school?"* It is very tough to answer this question in depth if you have not done the proper research on the college. (If you've read the chapter on selecting colleges, you should have already answered this.) You can also watch the videos a college has listed on their YouTube channel to find out things that make this college unique. Compare your school to other schools and decide what makes this school distinct to you. Review the chapter on shopping for colleges because it will give you a basis for understanding the difference between one school and another. When you answer this question, have at least seven bullet points for why you are interested in this school and make sure to answer it in a practical way. For example, if you say,

> When I was looking for colleges, I wanted to find a school in a city that I have never lived in that also has academic programs that can challenge me. I chose NYU because it is near my family, and it allows me to get internships in advertising. There are many different majors and courses that I can try. There are students from all over the country and the world that I can interact with, the academic standards are high, and I can see myself living in New York City. Also, I feel comfortable knowing that there are other Jewish students that attend, so I know I will be among peers.

This is an okay answer; it's practical and a good starting point. What you don't want to say is a bunch of fluff that shows you clearly don't know what the school has to offer. What is worse is if you've simply copied lines from their marketing materials like this:

> NYU offers a rich academic and cultural environment and a place I can call home. Its tall buildings and unique architecture would provide me with inspiration and a chance to feel like I can start a new beginning.

This answer has no in depth or explanation. It seems insincere.

Write the way you talk. It's okay to write your essay like a conversation and make it more formal as you go along. You don't have to and you shouldn't write this essay like it is a research paper with very little personality. Writing with super fancy language is sure to make the reader get bored or fall asleep because your essay requires focused effort to read instead of allowing readers to fall through the piece. They should never realize how many words they just read.

Try several approaches to the prompt. Use a few different approaches to answering the question. You can try answering the prompt head on (i.e. "Yes I agree", or "no, I disagree and here's why") or with a narrative that has a moral to the story. You can also play around with the chronology that you use when telling the story. Think of movies that start at the end and work backwards; they're intriguing. When you approach answering an essay, you want to think about how most people would answer the prompt. The easiest way to do that is to ask the people in your life how they would answer the question. However, don't forget that there is key information that you are trying to convey. Ultimately after reading your essay, readers should feel like they are hearing from a student who demonstrates the following:

Maturity: The student seems to have a good head on his shoulders, has learned life lessons, and can look back at his life and identify when he was thinking like a child versus thinking like an adult.

Humility: Although the student has a lot going for her, she still has her feet on the ground and can respect someone else's wisdom and understand that she still has a lot to learn.

The ability to tell a story: The student can walk readers through a series of events and keep them engaged. He should make his point or reach the punch line cleverly.

Well thought out ideas: The student really thinks about her answer and addresses counterarguments when she writes. She plays her own devil's advocate.

Critical thinking skills (challenge assumptions): The student does not accept assumptions at face value, but rather, tries to explore the assumptions and determines whether they are true before answering.

The ability to answer the question: The student can stay on topic and answer the question he was asked in a satisfactory manner.

The ability to support an argument: The student provides proof or evidence to support her argument, especially evidence that can speak for itself.

Uniqueness: Someone who can cut through all the fluff and clearly answer what makes them unique will fit the bill. She can show a combination of attributes that would be very hard to find in someone else, especially without needing to sit with an interviewer or fact finder who is good at uncovering rare and remarkable traits in a student.

Tenacity and competiveness: The essay shows, not tells, us how the student reacts when he experiences failure or competition. It shows a sense of determination and vigor when this person experiences challenging situations.

Ambition: The student can visualize something that seems impossible and takes steps to make this dream a reality. They dream big and have lofty goals.

A positive outlook on life: The student feels like the world is a good place, but some bad things can happen. They aren't cynical, but they aren't unreasonably optimistic either.

If a college requires more than one essay, all your essays should cover a breadth of topics. After reading all of your essays, the admissions boards should know how well you can address a range of topics. Use different styles and approaches in your writing to showcase your skills. They should be able to imagine having coffee with you and having a stimulating conversation that makes them think of things they've never thought of before, or makes them think in a different way.

After reading the first draft of your essay, list the characteristics and use that list as a rubric to see how effective your essays and applications are.

Topics To Avoid

Depression: The university has to be able to envision you in a new environment where you will have to make new friends and be faced with challenges you have never faced before. If you talk about periods in your life where you were deeply depressed, even if the situations really warranted a period of depression, it makes them wonder if you can handle their campus. I would avoid this topic except in very rare cases.

Situations in which you consider yourself a victim: You want to present yourself as someone who rises to the occasion and takes responsibly for life and actions. If you write about a situation where something happened to you that you could not do anything about, make sure you don't use it as a crutch or story as to why you cannot do something. If you do so, the essay typically will not do well. It is okay to talk about hardships. In fact it is recommended, but the worse the problem is, the better the ending/solution has to be. Think of it as a scale, with the problem on one end and the solution on the other. They need to be in balance.

Things you wouldn't want anyone to know. Don't write about anything you wouldn't want someone that has never met you before, to know. Most of the time, you will never get an opportunity to explain what you wrote to the admissions team. The reader doesn't know you and doesn't know if you are always like that or only when you're in a certain mood. If you're really smart and focused but you think deep down that you're lazy and disorganized, don't write an essay about how lazy and disorganized you are. The college is going to assume that you are like this all the time. At the very least, they're going to see you as someone who lacks self-confidence. They won't consider you as someone who is hard on themselves and can handle stress unless you point this out yourself.

Part Three: How To Position Yourself As A Scholarship Candidate

Chapter 18: What A University Wants

"Intelligence plus character —
that is the goal of true education."
— Martin Luther King, Jr.

I think it surprises people when they hear about students who get accepted to competitive colleges or universities without having equally competitive grades and test scores. Colleges are indeed looking at the grades and test scores, but they're really looking at the character behind the student with good grades and scores. Good grades and test scores are simply an indication of strong character, discipline, ambition and focus. This is why I'm often able to help students with some good character get scholarships to attend competitive schools regardless of their grades and test scores. It is also why I spend so much time working with students on their college essays. Our goal is to help this college to realize that the student has potential and leadership qualities any college or employer would want.

It's very seldom that parents, students, and even counselors start the application process considering this. They get so caught up in all the statistics that they forget what's behind the numbers. Furthermore, the extraordinary thing about the strategy of communicating character above mere grades and test scores is that with enough time, you can teach any student with character how to increase their grades and test scores by coaching them to overcome their bad study habits, test anxiety and lack of motivation and lack of goals. It just takes time so you have to start early.

Although you do need both character and academic promise to be successful in college, GPA just indicates a history of consistent discipline in high school. It doesn't mean a student with good grades in high school won't burn out in college, and it doesn't mean a student with low grades in high school has not matured enough to excel in college. You can't get into Harvard and Yale on character alone because you're competing against a pool of applications who have earned their stripes getting good grades for years, but you'd be surprised by how much character plays a role in college admission and scholarship awards at most other colleges.

If you don't have the high grades, high test scores or time to develop yourself as a candidate, you'll need to spend a great deal of time describing whatever else you can bring to the table or explaining your extenuating circumstances, such as taking care of your younger siblings while working a job and going to high school or independently learning photography or Italian. Explanations like these demonstrate potential and character to colleges.

While your life story may not sound as hard as someone else's, it serves you to explain anything you've had to overcome in life to set the context for your application. Most top colleges give you an extra 500 words to explain this in addition to your college essay. The truth is, if you have determination and drive, you will get into college. Someone is going to accept you because you deserve to be there—it's just a question of who. Besides many students have higher GPAs in college than they did in high school because they've matured.

I didn't have good grades until my senior year of high school, but I had character so I got into a college that normally wouldn't accept a student with my stats. Many of my clients are in a similar situation, so we work together to create a compelling argument as to why a college should accept a student despite his high school transcript and test scores.

This goes without saying but, although you can get a student into college without good grades and test scores, if you have time, you should strive to get the best grades and test scores you can. The reason for this is that when you don't have good grades and test scores, you're at the mercy of people who read your application. They are the ones that will decide whether they want to take a chance on you. Don't put yourself in this situation if you can help it. We'll talk about how you can raise your grades, test scores and qualifications in the remaining chapters.

A University Wants Character

I think many successful people would agree that a person's character tells them more about their potential than their intelligence. We all know very smart people that are not where they need to be for many of the reasons that will follow. Whether it's a lack of ethics, courage, discipline, or tenacity, we find that being smart is not enough to be successful. You have to have the heart. The traits below are not only enough to be a successful college-bound student, but they will help you become successful in life. When we teach our students how to get into college, it is really a "wax on, wax off" example. They learn how to approach every challenge in their lives, and we also help them to discover who they need to be in order to get the things that they want out of life. There will always be tips and tricks and techniques to game the system, just like there will always be people who will do anything to win, even at the cost of their own morality. What will never change, however, are the characteristics of a successful person. Sure, getting a scholarship to attend college can and will become more competitive, and parts of the admissions process will change, but one thing that's for sure is, a kid that has all the characteristics listed below will always find a college that is willing to pay for them to attend.

Drive and Determination

"If you stay at it, you have a 50/50 chance of making it, but if you give up you have a 100% chance that you will fail."
— Unknown

You must have a reason to be successful; goals, to put it simply. Without goals, your only motivation will be to avoid pain. As a result, if you don't have any immediate pains, you are trying to avoid, you will just become complacent. Right now your goal is to get into college. Before you make it there, you have to be able to answer why you want and deserve to go in the first place. If your reasons change or become irrelevant, that will throw a monkey wrench into your entire plan. College planning is not just about wanting or thinking you are entitled to go to college; you also must be willing to put forth the effort to get there. Good things don't come without sacrifice; you must decide what you are willing to give up to be in the 33% of Americans who have earned a college degree. Fundamentally, you must believe that if you work hard enough and are patient, you will get what you want out of life.

Curiosity And A Passion For Learning

"When the student is ready the teacher will appear."
— Buddhist Proverb

Learning should be fun. You have to find joy in learning because the truth is, you'll be learning until you die. You are a student, first of academia, then of life skills, and then, your career. Right now being a student is your occupation. Think of it as if you are a professional learner who is getting paid to learn, or who will soon be getting paid tens, if not hundreds of thousands of dollars from colleges to study at a university. You should enjoy it and accept that you will be learning for a long time, so you might was well get good at it. Don't just study what people tell you to study. Study what you want to know. I need you to read that again: _Don't just study what people tell you to study. Study what you want to know_. All the information is out there and if you make it your intention to discover it, you will find a teacher.

Courage In The Face Of Failure

"You cannot succeed without that possibility of failure."
— Michael Jordan

You are going to fail. It sounds cynical, but it is the truth. Many people think that the path to success is a straight line, but what most successful people know is that the path is more like a zig-zag that finally ends at your destination. Successful people try _until_ they succeed and accept that they will fail. Accept that if you try ten things, you may only succeed at one or two. Just remember, the person who did not even try will never have the same amount of success as you, especially in the long run.

Morals and Ethics

"Be true to the game. And the game will be true to you. If you try to shortcut the game, then the game is going to shortcut you. If you put forth the effort, good things will be bestowed upon you. That is truly about the game and in a lot of ways about life."
— Michael Jordan

There are many people that are intelligent but lack morals and integrity. Many of these people were awarded great opportunities in education and life but lost these opportunities because they were not ethical. What this really means is that they made decisions that showed little or no regard for others. Don't do that. Live your life by a moral code of what is right and wrong. Consider the consequences of your actions and reflect on them, not just about what would happen to yourself or even another

181

person you know, but what would the world be like if everyone did this. Don't use your intelligence to learn how to cheat, steal, manipulate or do something that calls for disciplinary action because of your own irresponsibility or recklessness. Command a higher standard for yourself even if you see others take the easy way out.

Discipline & Focus

"To all the dreamers out there keep dreaming,
but sometimes you have to
wake up from a dream and go get it."
— Sean Combs

Discipline is always something that you feel better about doing when you're looking back and are proud of where you've come. However, with discipline comes every distraction in the world. Everything comes up; every person wants to requisition your time, energy, and attention. You will be tested and it will be hard to keep your determination. Turn off your phones and ignore your email. Disable your text and social media notifications on your phone and set up Internet blocks for Facebook, YouTube, and any other sites you waste time on when it's time to focus. Remember what you're supposed to be doing and notice when you are being distracted. The following is a quote from one of my mentors. He's retired and has been retired since he was 28 years old.

"Discipline is hard work that pays you
back in fulfillment. But what is fulfillment?
Fulfillment is the satisfaction, or happiness as
a result of fully developing one's abilities or
character. Discipline and focus is 70% of the
battle with yourself and 30% with the outside
world. You have to find a way to motivate
yourself to do things even when you don't
want to because you are trusting in your

182

higher self. This higher self knows what is best for you and looks out for your future."
— James Rick Stinson

One of the secrets to my success is that I don't worry about what anybody else is doing. I don't spend time gossiping or talking about celebrities, and I really try to cut out the TV. I realized that by watching TV all day, all I'm doing is watching millionaires get paid because they can hold my attention. They have created something that makes me willing to give up time, energy, and focus that I could be directing to other tasks. The people on TV are really the ones pursuing their dreams while I sit in my living room on the couch doing nothing.

You get out of life what you put into it. The more you become committed to your dream and stay focused, the more help will arrive, the more people will respect you for having found your identity, and the more people will follow your leadership.

Authenticity and Sincerity

"Be you. Don't try to be different."
— Unknown

Don't try to be like everyone else. Don't put on a facade of what you think you are supposed to be or sound like. Colleges are looking for diversity and people with new experiences and ideas to bring to the classroom. If you're focused on being a cookie-cutter applicant, you'll only look like a commodity. What is rare is someone who is genuine, sincere, humble and honest. For example, don't try to use big words on your essays because you think that's how a Stanford man is supposed to sound. A highly intelligent person should be able to communicate any idea to a child, at least the fundamental principle of it.

Don't try to copy what everybody else does to get into college. Look at examples, see what is necessary to compete, and then go over what is important and see what you can bring to the table. Trying to copy what someone else did to get into Princeton is counterproductive. College admissions' personnel are looking at hundreds or thousands of applications that all sound the same. You want to stand out because human beings are attracted to what is unique and different in a significant way.

This is a very important concept in branding, which is what you're doing. You are essentially a personal brand to these colleges. People buy Apple products because they look different, work differently, and offer a unique experience when you use them. That's why you can still see people lined up outside the stores, even during a recession. They get the buyer's attention because they are unique, and the buyer wants a closer look. What's unique about you? What kind of unique experience can you take someone through when reading your essay and reviewing your college and scholarship application? What are they going to remember about you? How are they going to feel when they meet you? Answer these questions, and you will uncover your personal brand. Be like Apple, show that you're unique and don't try to look like every other applicant.

Patience & Persistence

"The strongest of all warriors are those two —
time and patience."
— Leo Tolstoy

You never know when your golden opportunity is going to show up, and you never know how much discipline and focus you will need to see progress. The truth is, good things take time to happen and develop. If you approach life with the mindset that you will only put forth effort if you see immediate results, you are likely to experience many humbling, and perhaps depressing disappointments. You will also have difficulty maintaining your drive during the ebbs and flows of life. This is because you are becoming too outcome-dependent instead of process-oriented. And you may be unwilling to admit how much you actually need to improve and are just assuming that you only need a few quick fixes to become a massive success.

Instead of wanting yourself to be successful already, become at peace with the fact that you are doing all that is necessary to reach your goals and enjoy the journey. There was a book I read, but I've forgotten the name, in which a young man and his father were hiking up a large hill. The child continued to ask, "Are we at the top of the hill, Dad? Are we there yet?" If we take a step back, we realize that the point of a hike is not to get to the top of the hill but to enjoy the hike itself. This is how you should approach being a college-bound student. This is part of who you are and this is what you do. Don't just focus on the end goal; enjoy each day as you put forth some effort towards your dreams. Eventually you will get there.

These days you have to approach someone with a proposal more than once just to get their attention. Many people are eliminated simply because they only asked once or they accepted the first "no" they received. For many people it is just easier for them to say "no" than to say "yes," but if this is something you need, want, or think is vital to your success, you must be persistent. Keep this in mind when you approach every part of the college process. You will hit roadblocks, setbacks, policies, and you will have to deal with difficult people. Don't let that discourage you. You know what you are going after and if you can't get their support yet, move on. They are likely to give it later once they realize that you are serious about what you're trying to do. A good example of this is when I tell you that you must enroll in college-bound courses. There will be many teachers and counselors who will tell you that you will not be able to pass the class. You have to make it clear to them that you have made this decision to challenge yourself, and you are going to do whatever it takes to rise to the occasion. It might take more than one conversation but that's persistence. Persistence is hard to ignore. It won't get you everything in life, but many doors that were once shut in your face will open up just because you showed some persistence. Persistence differentiates you from the average student and shows that you are really serious and you care. Don't take "no" for an answer.

As mentioned before, 31.9% of Americans have a bachelor's degree or higher. That means 68.1% of Americans do not. Remember, the opportunity to get an education is a gift. There are many American and international students that universities had to reject to give you an opportunity. Maximize this opportunity. Have the tenacity to overcome life's challenges. Someone is always watching. Like I said before, very seldom do people succeed on the first try. Always be willing try a different approach and push yourself. Don't be stagnant. Take the breaks you need but keep your feet moving. Don't go backward, and don't move laterally. Life is like a video game that gets more difficult the better you get at it. Keep moving forward. Nothing is going to stop you from getting what you want out of life if your intentions are virtuous. Just have the patience.

Influence & Interpersonal Skills

"To be persuasive we must be believable; to be believable we must be credible; to be credible we must be truthful."
— Edward R. Murrow

So now that you are practicing all the characteristics of a great student, you have to communicate what makes you great to someone who can make a decision for you. Understand who you are talking to and what motivates them. Put yourself in their shoes. Everyone wants to feel appreciated and respected. Find out what this person wants.

Understand the outcome of what you are trying to ask them to do and make sure that it is clear. For example, "by the end of this meeting, I want to make sure that this person knows that I am capable of handling an AP class" is a good thing to remember when you are trying to talk to a counselor about your classes.

Every teacher wants a good pupil. Everyone wants to be part of a success story. Everyone wants to help out a humble person who just wants to make something of himself or herself. However, keep in mind that you cannot influence someone if you are judging them long term. If you don't like your teacher, you will have a hard time influencing them to do anything for you. Keep the following ideas at the forefront of your mind as you interact with your teachers, counselors, and advisors. It will go a long way in getting you the decisions that you need.

1. Show that you value the person's advice and opinion.
2. Know who they are, the power that they wield, and how they can help you.
3. Everyone wants to be listened to and understood.
4. Sell your capabilities before you sell any of your ideas.
5. No one will listen to a word you have to say unless they know you care about them and they know what your motivations are. Take time to think this through.
6. Don't gripe or complain.
7. Don't try to explain away your mistakes. Take responsibility.
8. Be honest, but not brutally honest.
9. Think about how you would feel if someone said to you what you said to them.
10. Don't be critical. Be understanding.

11. Don't cut people off when they are talking to you. You must force yourself to find what they say interesting; understand what they know and what their concerns are. You cannot influence them unless you know this.
12. Appreciate every opportunity you've been given. Say "thank you," and write thank you letters.
13. Deliver what you said you were going to deliver.

Maturity

"The greatest day in your life and mine
is when we take total responsibility for our attitudes.
That's the day we truly grow up."
— John C. Maxwell

In college, there's nobody to wake you up to make sure you go to class. You can go an entire semester without showing up to class at all, and most universities won't send a letter to your parents. You don't get a report card in the traditional sense, and your grades aren't mailed to your house. There is no one to watch over you and keep you on track except yourself. You must take responsibility for your own education. When you get sick, you must be able to take care of yourself. You must prevent yourself from being distracted. There is no one to ground you or take the TV out of your room so you can study. You must have power over yourself and demonstrate this so that a college will know that you are not just going to be someone who drops out because they can't handle being on their own.

Understand and appreciate the opportunity you have. I don't know if there is a finite number of opportunities that each of us gets in our lifetime, but seize as many as you can without spreading yourself too thinly. Respect each opportunity as a stepping stone to the next one, and realize that no one's life is smooth and perfect.

Has a Broad Range of Intellectual Interests

"I divide all readers into two classes: those who read to
remember and those who read to forget."
— William Lyon Phelps

Part of what makes someone a highly influential
person is being able to handle a conversation with all types
of people. You'll find that many people have a hard time
relating to someone when they don't have anything in
common. Part of engaging in higher education is so you
can have a solid foundation of topics you can speak
intelligently about. Whether you decide to become a
professor or go into a profession after graduation, a well-
rounded education makes you a good citizen by enabling
you to make informed voting decisions. You must have the
capacity to understand all of the challenges of life. Majors
were created because the specialized knowledge is useful to
solve a problem in society. You can appreciate someone
who has studied and mastered any particular subject if you
have studied a portion of it yourself. For example, if you're
a business major and your eyes glaze over when there's a
lecture about biology, you are missing the point of having
an education. You may limit your opportunities because
you were not aware of what is out there. When you get into
the real world, you can lose out on a job in the business
section of a pharmaceutical or biotechnology company
because you weren't paying attention in class when the
topic was taught. Scholars understand humanities, math,
science, social sciences, rhetoric, arts and languages. You
need to be well-rounded.

Have an interest in new cultures, and bring forth
awareness and tolerance. There are so many things to learn
in this world. We need someone who is interested in
pushing a body of knowledge forward. The more you are
exposed to different ways of life, the more you understand
yourself and appreciate what you have. You will always

encounter people who believe differently than you. That's what makes the world so great. It's an asset to have an interest in understanding someone else's culture and an appreciation for their perspective and difference of opinion. Human beings always fear what they do not understand, so part of being a scholar, and a leader in society, is the ability to shed some light on a topic for other people.

Leads, Encourages & Supports Their Peers

"When someone praises us and talks about our good qualities, we become happy. Since everyone else also enjoys receiving such praise, we should be happy when this happens too. It is only our senseless jealously that deprives us of feeling pleasure when others receive praise."
— Geshe Kelsang Gyatso

The more people you help, the more successful you will be. This is not a zero sum game. If we cooperate, we can create more than by ourselves. Part of being a leader is the ability to be the rock and resource to your peers, friends, and family. You must give back and pay forward. You have to help yourself before you help other people so that you can continue to support others. However, keep in mind that many kind people have supported you to get you to where you are. You must pay it forward.

Show initiative to solve current problems. There will always be problems and things we can improve on. Instead of griping and complaining about how things are, take the initiative to suggest and make improvements once you have a foundational understanding. Do not be too quick to try to outshine your teacher until you have adequately learned from this person. Once you've learned all you can know, now you can innovate. With your education you can solve the problems that people before you could not.

Work on yourself before you work on other problems beyond your own. The best you can do for everyone is to be your best self, and then you can help.

There are so many issues in the world that we need educated people to solve. As part of your purpose as a student and part of the community of educated people, it is your civic duty to provide your gifts to the world.

Someone Who Contributes To Their Community

"There is no exercise better for the heart than reaching down and lifting people up."
— John Holmes

There are people in your community that cannot read, count, speak English, or do simple math problems. There are people that do not have access to the resources that you have. Part of us giving you the opportunity to get an education is for you to improve your community by being an informed, capable citizen that sets an example for others.

Be someone who can share your unique understanding of the world with others as you become more educated. You're educated now, but as you become more educated, you will start to develop a unique perspective. Sometimes you will find that your way of looking at a problem is different enough to make a breakthrough in society just because you're approaching the problem from a different angle or philosophy. For instance, your idea of justice and human rights may become clearer when you go to other countries or study different human conditions. You may already have experiences that allow you to have a unique outlook on life. It is your job to not only share it, but to be educated and influential enough to communicate these ideas to others.

"Every adversity, every failure, every heartache carries with it the seed of an equal or greater benefit."
— Napoleon Hill

The one thing that no one is willing to accept is someone who has a cynical outlook on life, especially when he or she passes on this cynicism to the rest of the world. It is very hard to be motivated and enthusiastic around people like this because they tend to shoot down ideas that could be great with a little more development. You want to believe that all people are good and that while there are some bad apples out there, and some things wrong with the system, life is good.

Happiness in life is important. And not all intelligent people are happy. Don't cling to your sob story or treat yourself like a victim of a circumstance. We all have a story and we all have reasons as to why life can be difficult for us. However, the person who is noteworthy is the person who succeeds despite the challenges of life because they have chosen not to make their challenges a limitation. Go through situations and hope for the best, but be practical. Consider the downsides and have alternatives if something doesn't pan out. And be sure not to become stagnant out of fear.

A University Wants Academic Promise

First of all, I hope I've made it clear that if you embody the characteristics in the above section and can communicate them well, there will definitely be a school willing accept you and give you a scholarship. Secondly, I hope you can agree that someone who has mastered the above characteristics is very likely to have all of the other factors that a university is looking for as long as someone told them what factors and metrics the colleges use to evaluate applicants. I've briefly discussed the metrics that colleges use to evaluate candidates, but we now will discuss this in far more detail. I left this section of the book until the end because you really only have between your 7th to 11th grade years to work on these things.

Below is a list of the most important academic factors colleges evaluate in order to make a decision about who to admit from the thousands of applications. These factors are more objective than the previous characteristics, and you do need to have both the academic background as well as character to get into colleges.

College Prep Courses

Metric: Weighted GPA

Not all high school courses are created equal. In most schools, the students are stratified by those who take all college-bound classes, some college-bound classes, regular classes, and vocational classes. The colleges that you apply to will look at all of the classes you have taken from the 9th grade until your senior year, so you want to make sure that these courses are challenging. This factor allows admissions to tell you apart from someone who has good grades in easier classes.

Good Grades & Study Habits

Metric: Unweighted GPA

This tells colleges how many of your classes you earned "As", "Bs", "Cs", etc. It basically gives them a snapshot of where you stand as a student in your high school.

National College Prep Exam

Metric: SAT, ACT, AP scores and SAT Subject Tests

These tests tell colleges how much knowledge you've gained compared to all the other students that are your age in the nation.

Feedback from Teachers & Mentors

Metric: Evaluation Score

These evaluations and comments tell colleges what you are like in the classroom and how you approach your education.

Leadership & Participation

Metric: Years in an activity, volunteer work hours, and/or work experience

Informs the admissions department about what skills you have outside the classroom. It shows that you are well-rounded and can handle multiple obligations.

Personality & Intentions

Metric: Presentation, essay, application and interview

These show us how well you are able to influence others and your attention to detail. It displays your major characteristics. It demonstrates how you approach this process and how creative you can be within the parameters that were provided.

Interest and Research

Metric: Campus Visits, Information Sessions Attended, Phone Calls/Emails to Admissions Officers & Faculty

This section lets us know how much you value the opportunity to attend the colleges you're applying to and how intelligently you make major life decisions. It also tells who really wants you to do this, whether it's you or your family. It's basically how you can show that you know what you're getting yourself into.

Chapter 19: Why College-Bound High School Courses Are So Important

"It is not so very important for a person to learn facts. For that he does not really need a college. He can learn them from books. The value of an education in a liberal arts college is not learning of many facts but the training of the mind to think something that cannot be learned from textbooks."

— Albert Einstein

There is no way to write a book on how to prepare a student for college without going over how to prepare for college classes. Your performance in college-bound classes is perhaps the single most important determinant to your success in college, and the colleges know this. Many students try to avoid taking these classes in order to have an easier time during high school, but it often comes back to haunt them. Colleges are looking to see what you have learned in high school and how hard you pushed yourself. College classes are much harder than high school classes, so you need to demonstrate to the colleges that you can handle them.

You want to avoid too many non-academic electives. It's fine to take an elective or two in something that interests you, but the truth is, there is very little room in a college-bound student's curriculum to take classes that do not count towards any academic credit. The most important classes to take are four years of the most important academic topics: English, a foreign language, science, math, social studies, and fine arts. Four years of each subject is best because it essentially matches the kind of curriculum you would study your first two years in college as your general education (GE) courses. It shows you have a well-rounded education and that you can build off the previous year's teaching as the classes get harder.

Avoid senioritis; your grades should be consistent throughout high school. Do not follow your friends that have decided to make their senior year a cake walk. You may hear that junior year is your most important year and that most colleges cannot see your senior year grades. While that is typically true, the top colleges in America want to see your mid-year and final year reports which contain your senior year grades. They can also still see what classes you're taking during your senior year as a way to see if you will continue to challenge yourself in college. Many students have had their acceptance letters withdrawn, because they failed a senior year class. Don't let that be you. On the other hand, I have seen students who have demonstrated a change in their behavior; i.e., they have really good grades but they bombed the SAT or vice versa, and received extended deadlines to improve their grades or SAT/ACT scores in order to get a second chance at acceptance.

Recommended Courses

Math: In order to complete the math required to be a competitive math, science, medical, engineering, or business student you must take your first academic math class in the seventh grade, so that you can take Geometry your first year of high school. The competitive college-bound students will have completed their first year of Calculus before they graduate. There will be many students that will have gone beyond the first year of Calculus before they graduate high school. They will take courses like Calculus III, Linear Algebra, or Differential Equations.

Here is a typical list of recommended math classes.

1. Pre-Algebra (7th Grade)
2. Algebra I (8th Grade)
3. Geometry (9th Grade)
4. Algebra II (10th Grade)
5. Pre-calculus/Trigonometry (11th Grade)
6. Calculus I (AB)/ Statistics (12th Grade)
7. Calculus II (BC)
8. Beyond

Science: If you are going to be studying anything science-related, you need the curriculum below in high school:

1. Physical Science
2. Biology
3. Chemistry
4. Physics/Environmental Science
5. Anatomy & Physiology (if your school offers it)
6. Beyond

Humanities & English: A good English and humanities curriculum is much more flexible than math and science. It typically looks like this:

1. World Literature
2. American Literature
3. English Language
4. English Literature

Social Science: With social science, we can also be a little more flexible. However, if you're planning to major in History or Political Science, you must take all these courses and perhaps more if you can fit them into your schedule.

1. Geography
2. World History
3. US History
4. American Government & Politics

5. Macroeconomics
6. Microeconomics

Foreign Language: Be sure to have four years in the same language. If you want to change it, change it early. Stick with your language. Some of the most common languages to study are:

1. Spanish
2. Chinese
3. French
4. Italian
5. German
6. Japanese
7. Latin
8. Hebrew
9. Sign Language

Fine Arts: Make sure you are being taught this class traditionally and that you walk out with skills. These classes are supposed to be nearly as challenging as learning a sport or taking an English class. Anything less than that will be considered a non-academic elective.

1. Studio Art
2. Art History
3. Music Theory
4. Theater
5. Dance
6. Film

Academic Electives: Before you consider nonacademic electives, consider these academic electives. These classes will most resemble the electives you will take in college. Any of these electives show that you can handle a college course.

1. European History
2. Human Geography

3. Psychology
4. Computer Science
5. Comparative Government and Politics
6. Statistics
7. Environmental Science
8. Philosophy
9. World Religions

At many high schools in America, public and private, any of the classes I listed above can have up to four levels of difficulty. You want to lean towards the more difficult ones because most of the students taking these classes are the college-bound students. Remember, getting "Bs" and "Cs" in the more difficult courses is worth more than getting straight "As" in the less difficult courses.

Most Difficult Course Load: Dual Enrollment at a Community College

At many high schools, students are allowed to enroll concurrently in high school as well as their local community college. The course that you take at your local community college can be taken if the class is not offered at your high school. This is generally the case when you have become so advanced that your current high school does not have the resources to continue to support you in a particular subject.

However, you need to keep in mind that you are taking college level classes. Expect the classes to be very difficult. They will be equivalent to the level of classes you take in your first few years of college. You can take these classes over the summer or during the year, whatever fits your schedule. Remember, a "B" in these classes will be equivalent to an "A" at your high school.

Difficult: AP Classes & IB Classes

These courses are similar to college classes but not as difficult as an actual college course. In addition, unlike college, these classes are usually taught over one year instead of one semester or one quarter. Below is a current list of AP courses:

1. Human Geography
2. Microeconomics
3. Psychology
4. Studio Art: 2-D Design
5. Studio Art: 3-D Design
6. Studio Art: Drawing
7. Biology
8. Computer Science A
9. Music Theory
10. Calculus AB
11. Calculus BC
12. French Language and Culture
13. Italian Language and Culture
14. Spanish Language and Culture
15. Spanish Literature and Culture
16. English Literature and Composition
17. English Language and Composition
18. German Language and Culture
19. Japanese Language and Culture
20. Latin
21. Physics B
22. Physics C: Electricity and Magnetism
23. Physics C: Mechanics
24. United States History
25. Government and Politics: Comparative
26. Statistics
27. World History
28. Chemistry
29. Environmental Science

30. Government and Politics: United States
31. Macroeconomics

Below is a list of IB Courses: You want to take the Higher Level (HL Courses):

1. Theory of Knowledge
2. Biology
3. Physics
4. Mathematics
5. English A: Literature
6. English B
7. History
8. Visual arts
9. Economics
10. Chemistry
11. French B
12. Social and Cultural Anthropology
13. Chemistry
14. Geography
15. Business and Management
16. Norwegian A: Literature
17. German B

The more AP, IB or community college courses you take the better. You will look like more like a college-bound student to the admissions panel. Just don't get a grade lower than a "C." Having a lot of "Cs" or "Ds" is not good by any measure. If you've never taken an AP or IB course before, take one in your strongest subject. For instance, if you tend to do better in English or social studies, try AP English or AP World History. Just remember that these classes will take some getting used to. In many cases, this will probably be the first time you've ever had to actually study for a class and have some difficulty keeping up with the reading. You'll get used to it if you're just taking one.

Three or four AP classes your junior and senior year are enough to get into the top 100 colleges in the United States provided you have good grades. You'll want to know that taking more than four AP courses is considered a college curriculum. It definitely makes you look like a highly competitive student. The most AP, IB, and or community college courses I have ever seen one person take is eight. I don't recommend it. Four to five is more than enough. After that, we have to move onto other parts of your qualifications.

Medium: Honor's Classes

Honors' classes are considered medium difficulty in the admissions panel's mind. Sometimes they are worth about one credit more towards your GPA; sometimes they are not. So a "B" in this class can also be worth an "A" in a regular class, but not always—it depends on the college whether they weight your grades in these classes.

Standard: Regular Classes

You and your parents may hate me for this, but you want to take as few of these classes as possible. If your counselor doesn't that think you should take more difficult courses, you might improve your performance in the classroom and/or make it clear to the counselor that you're trying to be a college-bound student. It helps to talk to the teacher of the advanced class, and see if they will give you an opportunity. Persistence is key here.

Private School vs. Public School

All things being equal, taking two to four honors and AP/IB classes at a public high school will give you the same qualifications of a high school student at most private schools. However, colleges do look at high school rankings, so some public and private high schools are more competitive than others.

Now I Know What You're Thinking...

How in the world am I going to do all of this work? First of all, you want you play your own game and you will become more advanced as you go along. I've listed here the highest standard that you need to meet so that can you play the game at your level. You do not have to do everything, but you should know that at the most elite colleges in the United States, you will compete against students that have accomplished many of these goals. Next, we will go over how to handle coursework like this, and in later chapters we will go over what kind of time management skills are necessary to get good grades in these classes without giving up your teenage life.

Also I want to congratulate you on completing this chapter. It's not often that I get to reveal all at once what it takes to get into the best of the best colleges in the United States. It scares most students to find out what kind of work it takes, but you were up to the challenge, so I'm proud of you for that.

Chapter 20: Your Commitment To Getting Good Grades Is The Secret Sauce

"Education is a shared commitment between dedicated teachers, motivated students and enthusiastic parents with high expectations."
— Bob Beauprez

You must be committed to the goal of being a good student. Four years of high school is a long time, and there are plenty of opportunities to lose focus. You must look at every class you take as a challenge to get an "A." The grade you get on every single report card, progress report, quiz, exam, test, paper, and group project, including extra credit, you should take personally as a representation of your work. Each semester you should look at what classes you need to take in order to graduate and stand out. Set a goal for yourself as a target GPA and check yourself periodically by talking with the teacher about your progress to make sure that you get the grade you want. When you don't get the GPA you want, ask yourself what happened. Where were you spending your time? Then make the difficult decision to cut out the habits that are stopping you from becoming your best self. Do not give up, finish what you started. This isn't supposed to be easy and you're not always going to get it right the first time.

Chapter 21: Your Relationship With Your Teacher Will Give You A Higher GPA!

"I never teach my pupils; I only attempt to provide the conditions in which they can learn."
— Albert Einstein

Your relationship with your teacher will have an influence on your grade. You must have a good relationship with your teacher. It is not an option to fail at this. Do not be the young genius in the back of the room that's constantly contradicting the teacher in front of her class and expecting that, because you set the curve on the exam, you are entitled to an "A." Likewise, if you are putting forth a genuine effort and the teacher likes you, they can give you a better grade. You are kidding yourself if you think you can pass a class with flying colors these days without the teacher adoring you.

Your teacher is a human being. They can appreciate someone who is putting in effort. You should know that teaching is very high-level and arduous work that requires you to hold the attention of many people and deal with different personality types. It's not an easy job, and it doesn't pay a lot of money, so it requires hard-working and intelligent people who care more about making a contribution to society than getting rich off their intelligence. It is remarkable and valuable to find a teacher who can handle all of this and still teach with passion and enthusiasm, so you must be respectful.

Teachers long for recognition that they have devoted their career to giving you an education. Even if your teacher is not good at making things simple and easy to understand, you must still show your gratitude towards them for educating you. Whatever shortcomings they have, you must make up for by asking questions or conducting self-study. If a college asks you why you didn't get a good grade in a class, they don't want to hear that it was because your teacher was bad or you just didn't like them. The teacher already has this education. It's your turn to get an education from him or her. It is a zero sum game to blame your teacher for your grade. With that being said, try and get teachers that have good reviews over the teachers that don't have good reviews. It's easier to learn when you have a passionate teacher, but that isn't a requirement.

Don't let what I'm about to write encourage you to slack off, but the truth is, if you have a good relationship with the teacher you will get a better grade, especially in classes that require writing. I can't tell you how many times, I really deserved a "C", but received a mercy "B" or "A", because the teacher saw improvement as I progressed through the class. Likewise, I've also had times in my student career where I was able to set the curve on the exams without ever showing up to class because I would cram the material on my own time. However, even though I set the curve, the teacher ended up awarding me a "C" because the teacher did not like my attitude and because they wanted more participation from me to help enrich the class experience.

Your teacher will be more willing to give you extra help if they like you. I have had many teachers give me a crash course on their entire class, give me a full overview on what's going to be on an exam, or tell me exactly what they wanted to hear on a paper because they liked me. I've had teachers look over my paper and give me a preliminary grade and then told me what I needed to do to get an "A" on a paper because they liked me. Life is easier when the teacher likes you.

If your teacher likes you, they will be more willing to tell you when you're slipping up before it's too late. You can take all the help you can get. The easier it is for you to get an "A" in a class, the more you can do, and the more time you can spend on other things. You must always check with your teacher and ask them their honest opinion about what they think of you as a student.

You need to meet your teacher the first week of class to go over how the course is structured. We'll go more into that later in the book, so don't worry about it too much now. Doing this does three things. One, it tells the teacher that you are going to be one of her "A" students. Secondly, it allows you to understand the big picture of the class. Thirdly, it helps you befriend the teacher and sets up an open line of communication so they can write you a college recommendation letter later.

Sit in the front of the class. I know it might sound nerdy, but you want to sit in the front of every class you plan on getting an "A" in. Sitting in front forces you to pay attention and not fall asleep. It's hard to fall asleep when the teacher is looking at you every minute. I have a mentor who invented a technology that randomly records students in the classroom. The students have no warning before they are on camera in front of the whole class. Studies have shown that increases the students' retention partly because they don't want to be seen falling asleep in front of everyone. In addition, the teacher remembers the students that sit in the front of the class easier than they do the students in the back of the class. When they are grading your work, they will recall what you were like as a student. This tends to sway your grade. The students who sit in the front, and participate in class, get all the mercy. If the teacher is not getting any participation from anyone in the class, they will call on you to save the standard and integrity of the class. For instance, if the teacher is going over a reading and it is clear that no one in the class actually read the book, they will call on you to save the discussion. This is good! When you sit in the front of the class and seem like you are serious about getting an "A," participating and helping the teacher will go a long way towards that goal.

Many students who do not understand what you are doing may try to ridicule, tease, or tell you that you are making them look bad by participating. Ignore them. You're right; they're doing it the wrong way. It's up to them when or whether they will ever get it. Some of them will finally wake up and come around, but don't allow misguided people to influence you. If they can't handle you stepping up, that's their problem. Be proud of how intelligent you are. Let people know and don't hold back. There is no way that you're going to be stupid for anybody else's benefit. Be the leader that commands the best out of your peers rather than giving into a culture of mediocrity. When it comes to being a good student, they need to be like you, not the other way around. The fact is the best students are the most likely to get the best opportunities in life. Either they need to get with the program, or they're going to get a mediocre or failing grade. If they get amazing grades doing little to no studying, good for them but they can't keep that up forever. At some point, such bad habits of poor time management and focus will catch up to them. Unfortunately, when you make lifestyle changes, many others will feel threatened by what you're doing. Get used to this and make friends with the students who are also trying to get good grades.

Often times the teacher will bump their favorite student's grades up by a full grade. As I mentioned before, participation and having a good attitude can go a long way. Don't expect your teacher to bump your grade up because they like you and make sure that you don't rely on it. However, the fact is, if you do all of the things in this chapter, quite often you will experience having your grade increased by the end of the year. Enjoy it because it doesn't happen all the time. Sometimes you just have to tell the teacher that your objective is to get an "A," and ask them what you will need to do in order to accomplish that.

You want to get into the habit of participating now because as you become more advanced, class participation will become more and more important. In college, class participation can range between 5-50% of your grade. In high school, it's not as easily spelled out, but it still makes a difference. Participate, show some enthusiasm, and never make the teacher feel like you don't need them or that they are not a good teacher. Ask good, insightful questions that show that you are applying what you are learning. For instance, if you are taking AP Psychology and covering Sigmund Freud, and you've already covered the topic of rationalization, it's a good idea to give an example of what you rationalize. One, it's funny; two, your teacher will see that you are learning and applying the information; and three, he or she will like you for making the quality of the lecture or discussion better. There are many students that can get an "A" in the class without saying a thing and sitting in the back, but it's a risky strategy and it now bases your grade 100% on your performance. A day will come when you really need some help or an understanding teacher and they are less likely to go the extra mile if you don't put in the effort throughout the year. Get in the habit of doing this early.

Chapter 22: By Understanding How The Course Is Structured You'll Learn More & Have More Fun

*"Two basic processes of education
are knowing and valuing."*
— Robert J. Havighurst

We've talked about sitting down with your teacher to understand what direction the class is going and how they are teaching the class. This is a great way to introduce yourself to your teacher, but the main reason why you are doing this is because you are essentially trying to get the teacher to give you the bullet points of the class so that you can know what he or she wants you to walk away with. Inevitably, this will be the information they will test you on.

You need to know when the exams are, when the projects are, and what you need to walk out of that class knowing. Once you know the answers to these questions, put a calendar in your room that details major exam dates, or plug them into your phone's calendar function. Think about why the teacher structured the class that way. This is important, so you that you can understand when the class digresses and why.

If you don't understand how the class is structured, it is very easy to get lost, especially if this is not a class you are used to taking or if the teacher is teaching you how a body of knowledge has progressed. By understanding the structure of the course, even if you get lost, you know where you are, and you know what you still don't know yet. Always revert back to the big picture if you get lost or if you do not understand a concept. Go back to what you do know so that you can make sure you are not missing any critical points.

By understanding why you are studying a particular topic, you know how it relates to everything else. If you understand why you have to learn a topic, it's much easier to want to learn it so that you can use the information. The information may be simply a building block that will later lead you to understand more relevant material. For instance, you must learn anatomy in order to become a doctor. Make sure you understand the core fundamentals. Ask your teacher where these topics can be applied in real life, and take it upon yourself to apply what you've learned whether or not the analogies or applications are 100% realistic. Although we want to maximize our understanding of the topic, most of the classes that you are taking are introductory courses, so you're not going to learn too much that you will be called upon professionally to apply just yet.

You don't want to misunderstand anything fundamental because it's embarrassing. You must know all that you need to know so that you know what to ignore and so you don't gloss over something extremely fundamental, especially in math. If you understand that the teacher is going to build off of certain math techniques as he or she goes through the course, you want to know that ahead of time so you make sure you understand the building blocks before they move on.

I'm not big on flashcards because they encourage memorization rather than an understanding of the topic. That doesn't mean that they don't work, but that type of studying is not going to allow you to remember what you learned for other exams or more advanced classes. Lastly if you want to really remember what you've learned when you graduate, it's best to try to understand it fundamentally. Nonetheless, if I am using flashcards, I will lay out all my flashcards on the floor and try to group the flashcards by concept i.e. all the bones, all the body parts in the torso, etc. This allows me to rearrange how I look at the information, and by constantly approaching the topics in different ways you can really start to understand the big picture, what is fundamental, and what tends to be consistent in what you're studying. This is how you realize that, for instance, more than 50% of all humor is based on a play on words ("The quickest way to a man's heart is through his chest" — Roseanne Barr) or the element of surprise ("My grandfather is hard of hearing. He needs to read lips. I don't mind him reading lips, but he uses one of those yellow highlighters" — Brian Kiley). This is how you draw principles from a field of study. These are the fundamental principles of comedy. So, if we were to study comedy, what we would realize is that there is a structure to learning, writing, and performing comedy. As we learn each technique, we will end up with a series of tools that we can apply. Via these tools, you'll learn that many times, even when you don't know the answer, you can infer the answer. Oftentimes you'll be correct enough for the teacher to give you credit, especially on short answer questions.

If you actually understand the course, it's easier to apply and remember what you learned. Yes, you want to get a good grade on the test, but one day you will look back at high school and college, and you won't remember the grades you earned on exams. It's ideal to have the attitude that you need to study for what's going to be on the test, but you're really studying to understand the topic so that you can use it in the future. You never know what you're going to need to know later on in life. One day you'll thank your stars that you were paying attention in Biology or English class.

Chapter 23: How To Ace All Of Your Classes

"Perhaps the most valuable result of all education is the ability to make yourself do the thing you have to do, whether you like it or not."
— Thomas H. Huxley

Don't try to study every single detail of what's being presented. Follow the 80/20 rule. Eighty percent of the material you will be tested on will come from 20% of the information presented. For instance, if I were to teach you a sport like football and later give you an exam on it, there would be more questions about the quarterback, running back, and receivers than there would be about the offensive or defensive line. Sorry, football athletes, you know it's true.

Put yourself in the teacher's shoes and consider what information your teacher would lose their job over if they gave you an "A" without knowing. For example, if you walk out of a Chemistry class and you still don't at least have a basic understanding of stoichiometry, atoms, molecules and ions, frankly you do not deserve an "A" or "B" in that class. Look at the learning objectives in the book or get them from the teacher. When you look at the syllabus, lectures, notes, and reading, ask yourself what the most important 20% of the information is to determine what you must know when reviewing for an exam.

Sometimes, especially in high school, you will have teachers that presumably want to test you on every little detail or word in the chapter. You'll find that once you understand the big picture, it doesn't seem like that anymore, but sometimes it can happen. Even if they want to test you on everything, you must study the 20% first before you get to the rest of the material. In most cases, you will get at least a "C" if you know the learning objectives for the class, and perhaps you may get an additional question or so correct because of reading the text or studying a special graphic or diagram in the book. Teachers will always say that you have to know everything, but it's just not possible to test you on everything. Sometimes they just throw you a curveball or two to see how much you've read and to separate the "A" students from the "A+" students. I was once a tutor for the athletes at my college for a class I was taking along with them. I just took better notes and studied the most important 20% of the information before they did and then taught that to them. The information that I presented them with was simply the essentials for review which would be enough to get a least a "C." Then to get an "A," I would go back through the details. Sometimes you can get an "A" just by studying the fundamentals, but you shouldn't rely on it. We use this as a foundation so you don't miss anything important, and it'll give you a safety net so you'll always pass the class. From there you keep drilling down.

Chapter 24: To Be A Consistent "A" Student – You Must Be Very Organized

"If you are planning for a year, sow rice; if you are planning for a decade, plant trees; if you are planning for a lifetime, educate people."
— Chinese Proverb

Remember that in a few short years, you will be taking a full semester course in which 40-100% of your grade could come down to just a few exams. These exams will take place in the middle or toward the end of the class. Unless you have a photographic memory, you cannot remember everything for a midterm or final. To prepare for this, you must put your notes in a format that you can quickly access and that allows you to look at them in a short period of time. Our approach to studying has you gradually add to your study guide as you go through the class to come up with a complete study guide before the exam. If all your notes are on loose-leaf paper that you can't find when it's time to study for the final, the test experience will become a disaster. Keep all your notes in one place and make sure your notes, quizzes, and so forth are held in that safe place. Don't ever throw away quizzes or exams even if you failed them. You can use them to review what you got wrong and what you still need to learn.

Use a binder, spiral notebook, file on your laptop, or whatever you need to keep track of all your notes when you need them. Each chapter should have its own tab, post-it or folder. If you are covering 18 chapters in the class, you should have at least 18 tabs, post-its or folders. Look at the syllabus to see how many chapters you are covering. When you meet with your teacher for the first time you should review your syllabus.

When it came time for me to study for a final, I just pulled out of my binder all the chapters I would be tested on. All the notes, quizzes, homework and problems were in there, and I could just consolidate them to figure out what's going to be on the test.

Chapter 25: The Art Of Taking Good Notes

"Training is everything. The peach was once a bitter almond; the cauliflower is nothing but a cabbage with a college education."
— Mark Twain

When the teacher says, "That's important, you should write that down," write it. Star it, underline it, highlight it, and do whatever you need to do so it stands out from all your other notes. Anything the teacher emphasizes and says is important is definitely fair game on the test. Even if you think it's stupid, they will find some way to test you on that material. Always ask yourself, why is he or she telling me this?

If you understand the big picture, taking good notes is easier to do because you will notice when your teacher is explaining something they told you that you would learn. Live and die by your learning objectives on the syllabus. When the teacher says, "In this lesson you should learn…," write it down every single time. When in doubt you can write down as much as you want. Don't write down every word because then you'll be overwhelmed when it comes time to study. However, if you don't understand something the teacher said, write it down verbatim, if possible, so you can review it later. Do the same thing if you're lost, and the class is moving quickly. Write it down and ask questions later.

I recommend taking notes in such a way that you can see all the notes from one lecture in a few pages. Rather than highlighting or writing something on each line, you want to write your notes so that they are sectioned off by concept. For example, if you were taking notes from this book, you would want to write:

How to do take good notes
- Remember learning objectives.
- Record what the teacher says is important.
- When in doubt, write it down.

It makes it easier if you can just go over your class notes, circle a few sections, and say, "That's definitely going to be on the exam." Eventually, you will have many sections with headings like this. You should circle the most important information and transfer them to your exam review cheat sheet.

Let's say you have notes from 16 different chapters, and each chapter has about 15 different headings like the one above. You will want to go through each lecture and circle about seven to nine sections of the most important ideas in those notes. This is how you can find and focus on the most important 20% of the information.

Chapter 26: How To Learn The Most In The Least Amount Of Time

"The ultimate goal of the educational system is to shift to the individual the burden of pursuing his own education."
— John W. Gardner

Review your notes after every lecture and before the next lecture or discussion. You'll find that if you don't do this, it will be much harder and take much longer to study for the inevitable midterm or final. Learn it along the way. Don't cram.

Once you have circled all the most important sections of each chapter, you need to consolidate all your notes on to one sheet of paper for each exam you have. You might be consolidating 16 chapters into about 60–100 concepts. That's far too many concepts to remember, so you want to look at the top 12-20 concepts to study first, i.e., the top 20%. Once you've remembered all of the most important concepts, then you can go back and review the rest of them.

You need to keep a record of previous quizzes and exams, so you can get a feel for what kinds of questions your teacher likes to ask. Do they favor multiple choice over short answer? Will you have an essay question? When you know what types of questions your teacher asks, it's easier to know what and how to study. There's nothing like knowing what your teacher is more likely to ask on a quiz. It's like being able to read his or her mind. You might find that they like to test your understanding of the intricacies of the subject and broad concepts, or memorize important little lists. Maybe they want you to apply the information to a problem or test your vocabulary? Once you've figured out what they like to test you on, studying and note taking will become easier.

Your notes and documents will be crucial when it's time for your final exam. As I mentioned before, when it was time to study for the final, I brought all the previous exams, notes, and quizzes together. It took me up to six hours to study for the final depending on how much I'd been paying attention all semester. While six hours of study may seem like a lot to you, many of my peers pulled all-nighters to review the same material and did not get better exam scores than I did. It looked like I was a genius.

If you understand the big picture, memorization becomes less and less important. However, every once in a while you will need to memorize a list of information or a detailed process like photosynthesis or what it takes for congress to pass a bill. In these situations you want to lay the list out and use acronyms, i.e., in Algebra the order of operations is PEMDAS (Please Excuse My Dear Aunt Sally). Practice a few and find what works for you. If acronyms don't work for you, visual pictures are another method to help you remember. For instance, when I was learning the vocabulary words for the SAT, I used a book called *Vocabulary Cartoons* that helped me to learn the word "tenacious." The book shows a man with an intense look on his face playing tennis, tenaciously. I was able to remember the word because of the image. The more extraordinary your memorization tool, the easier it will be to remember later.

Rewrite your cheat sheet three times. It seems excessive, but you must keep rewriting this sheet until you can do it from memory. If your notes truly reflect what will be on the test, then you will have information memorized. Everything you need to know from the test will be on the cheat sheet, but what you will realize is that it's not the cheat sheet that makes the test easy. It's the process you took to make it. Other people will see your cheat sheet and think if they just copied it, they will get the same grade as you. Not true.

Chapter 27: How To Know What's Going To Be On The Exam Without Cheating

"The carefully fostered theory that schoolwork can be made easy and enjoyable breaks down as soon as anything, however trivial, has to be learned."
— Agnes Repplier

Provided you've followed the directions in the previous chapters and have created and reviewed, your study sheet, you've now completed half the battle for test preparation. Now you have to actually take them. The very first thing you want to do is write down key points that you'll need to remember the minute the test starts. Take a look at all the questions, and jot down a few notes about the topics before you even answer one question. It's a good strategy because you can forget key information as the test continues. When you write concepts and formulas down at the beginning, you have something to go back to and look over.

Once that's done, go through and answer every question that you know the answer to. This allows you to get those easy questions out of the way, so you have more time to focus on the harder ones. For the rest of the questions, you want to make sure you really understand them before you start answering. If you don't, get up and go ask the proctor. A lot of the times that proctor will give you a clue that makes your life much easier and possibly even allows you to infer the answer. Choose the answer that seems the truest and is the most congruent with the questions. If you studied, you'll have enough of an understanding to know when an answer choice could be right. Otherwise, use the process of elimination and go with your gut. Sometimes the questions on one part of the exam will help to answer a question in another part of the test. A teacher will seldom test you on the same concept twice, so if you know that you already answered a question on that topic, go back and make sure you really understood the question.

Chapter 28: How To Write "A" Papers Every Time

"To defend what you've written is a sign that you are alive."
— William Zinsser

Exams and participation are only part of your grade. The other part comes from papers. Check with your teacher regarding each paper, so you can go over the concept. If your teacher has given you a prompt, and you think you have a good answer, run it by them and let them know how you will go about building your argument. They will give you feedback, so you can see if you are on the right track. They can also let you know how they would prefer you answer the question. If they tell you what they prefer you write, make sure to address that in your paper. They are the ones giving you the grade so give them what they asked. Think of it as them telling you exactly what they want for Christmas. If they don't tell you what they want you to address, make sure you at least understand the prompt. When in doubt about what to write, go back to your notes and see if the teacher ever gave you clues of how to answer this question.

Make sure you demonstrate an understanding of the subject matter by applying what you learned in class. Most of the time, especially in a social science class, a teacher might tell you to write a paper on a broad topic like the history of the presidency. This is time to use the concepts, vocabulary, and jargon you've learned, but make sure you really understand those words and concepts. The teacher wants to see that you have an enhanced perspective based on what they have taught you. They've usually given you a question that tests your use of the perspective or analytical tools they've addressed.

Your grade on your paper will, most of the time, come down to the quality of your writing. You'll find that a well written essay is hard to not give an "A" to, unless the writer is eloquent but clearly does not understand the subject matter. Once at my college there was a student that was just sitting in an economics course to accompany his friend. He had no background in economics but he was just a great writer. He took the exam with everyone else and just because he had such a well thought out answer and well written paper he got a "B" on the exam.

Chapter 29: How To Use Study Groups To Make You Smarter

"Every successful individual knows
that his or her achievement depends
on a community of persons working together."
— Paul Ryan

Make sure you get the contact information of your peers in the class. You never know when you will completely forget about an exam, get sick and miss a crucial lecture, or just can't get the answer to a math question. Doing it yourself is good but sometimes, you will need help. Study groups can help with that. Study groups are great resources; they can help you review concepts right before a test or go over different points when discussing a reading. Everyone has studied and they're just reviewing major concepts with each other to make sure that they understand everything. It helps to see how other students remember the information or what their opinion is of what's going to be on the test. However, you need to be able to study on your own so you can bring some content to the group. No one likes it when they have to do all the work and bring all the information while everyone else slacks off. Your study buddies should be students that are sitting next to you in the front of the class. If they are not, just make sure that you don't join a study group in which you are the most informed person in the group. There is a time and place to teach others and apply what you learned— namely, the day of the test—but you're not supposed to be teaching in a study group. You're supposed to be reviewing what you all have studied. If you feel you are carrying the team, find another group or make the other students focus on specific topics.

Chapter 30: Using A Tutor Is Not Cheating

"Better than a thousand days of diligent study is one day with a great teacher."
— Japanese Proverb

For a few, some subjects are naturally easier to learn than others. Seek help in the subjects you don't know well. You'll know when it's time to seek help if you're trying to understand something you've adequately studied, but still have a hard time grasping. When this happens, don't waste any more time. Ask someone that can explain it in a few seconds, i.e., a tutor.

The tutor's job is to clear up things that you're having trouble with, not present your subject matter to you as if you are learning it for the first time. You learn something when you find out what the big picture is, what the "must know" points are, the fundamental principles (what the subject all comes down to), and what you must truly understand. Do not rely on a tutor to totally teach a subject or expect them to spoon-feed you the information. You are setting yourself up to always rely on another person to learn something. As the late Jim Rohn said, "You can't hire someone else to do your push-ups for you." *You* have to learn. It's your education.

Chapter 31: How To Turbo Boost Your SAT & ACT Scores

"It is important to have the student demonstrate that he has developed a degree of intellectual competence rather than that he has acquired a certain number of semester credits."
— Detlev V. Bronk

Your SAT and/or ACT scores will make a significant difference in which schools you get admitted to. The hardest schools to get admitted to are the schools that have the most money. In order to get into them, you must have high SAT or ACT scores among other things. These scores are also a major determinant for merit-based scholarships. Not all schools give out merit aid but if they do, your SAT and/or ACT score will be one of the major things that they look at—if not the most important metric.

Getting a good SAT or ACT score takes practice. That's why I highly recommended that you start early. How early? You should be studying for the SAT or ACT no later than the second semester of your freshman year of high school. You are starting this early so you can be prepared to take the PSAT/NMSQT exam in your junior year. The PSAT/NMSQT exam can kick off your scholarship search and get colleges interested in you. It'll also prepare you for the actual SAT or ACT exam which is what colleges evaluate for college admission.

Many prestigious college prep high schools tell you not to think about the SAT and ACT exam until your junior or senior year. This is often because they want you to focus on your grades, but if you ask the average highly skilled test prep tutor, they always tell you to start earlier.

As of today the SAT is out of three sections: Writing, Critical Reading, and Math. The maximum score for each part of the exam is 800. To me, the hardest part of getting a good score on the SAT, besides practice, comes down to knowing the vocabulary needed to pass the critical reading portion. Secondly, it's memorizing all the formulas and procedures for the math problems. Take an SAT diagnostic exam as soon as you can so that you can see what your strengths and weaknesses are. Each section of the test will have easy, medium, and difficult questions. The diagnostic exam will let you know what questions you are missing. Missing a significant number of easy and medium questions means that there are fundamental things you need to learn or practice. If you are missing the difficult ones, then you will need to find resources to teach you how to approach the difficult parts of the exam. Budget a minimum of 80 hours to practice. You read that right: 80 hours. That's a little less than 3 and a half hours per week over a 6 month period or a little over one and a half hours per week over one year. It needs to be part of your routine.

Aim high. A 620 in each section will be enough to solidify your chances at one of the top 500 colleges in America and possibly receive some merit scholarships. If you have a 750, you can either be admitted to some of top 50 colleges in America or receive merit scholarships at nearly any university that is not among the top 25 colleges. The top 25 colleges do not usually offer merit unless your scores are nearly perfect, but once again, if you have any kind of financial aid eligibly, they will meet your eligibility generously.

The ACT Exam has four sections: English, Math, Reading, Science and Writing. The maximum score is 36 on the first four each sections. The maximum score on the Writing section is 12. A 28 on this exam is generally good enough to get a merit scholarship somewhere.

Personally I prefer the ACT over the SAT. Colleges accept both scores equally now. In fact, recent trends have shown that more people are taking the ACT than the SAT. The reason I prefer the ACT over the SAT is that the questions on the ACT are more straightforward. So if you've been taught the concept in class, you're likely to choose the correct answer on the ACT with less test-specific practice versus the SAT which often requires you to become familiar with how the test maker designs the test. For example, the ACT has more advanced Algebra II and Trigonometry questions, so it's useful to bring a graphic calculator to the exam, but the SAT exam is designed so no question requires a calculator if you have strong reasoning skills.

You will need resources to improve your score. Each type of resource is different; however, what's most important is how you use those resources and how much time you spend studying.

Practice Exams

The very first thing you should do is to go online and search for a free, official, retired exam made from the people who actually make ACT or SAT. You don't have to take the entire exam all in one sitting unless the test is coming up soon. You can just work on a section of exam until the specific testing time limit is met.

Always take both exams first, before you study either. Take at least one official SAT as well as one official ACT. You'll want to take a retired official exam first because it will give you the closest insight to how the test makers format their questions. Other test prep resources cannot plagiarize test questions, so they have to change it up a little which skews your expectations some.

Once you take the exam, you should score the exam yourself so you can see which questions you got wrong. You especially want to look for the questions in which the correct answer was your second choice. You probably overthought the answer, or maybe you had no idea what the questions were asking. This is very valuable insight and important to understand no matter how much time you have to study for the exam.

Test Prep Books

Once you have taken an exam and compare your SAT score to your ACT scores, you can consider another resource. The most inexpensive resources for test prep are SAT or ACT books. Not all books are equal. I prefer books that provide you with the study material, explanations and worked-out solutions, as well as tons of practice exams and questions. Any book that lays out all the different types of questions you may be asked one-by-one is good.

Make sure to take the diagnostic test in the book first. (NOTE: before this you should have already taken an official retired exam.) This part is usually at the front of the book and will give you an idea of what your weaknesses are. Study the lessons on your weakest sections first, and then move on to other parts of the book. Do not cram cover to cover with the book. Start with your weaknesses after you have completed their diagnostic set.

Software & Home-Study Courses

One step up from books are SAT or ACT prep software and home study courses. These courses are also very inexpensive, and some are free online. The beauty about software and the home-study courses are that most of them are very effective for any student who completes all the homework. You often get very high level instruction for a low cost. You must, however, be determined to finish or the course will just sit on your shelf and collect dust.

SAT & ACT Boot Camps
Or Live Trainings

If you don't think you'll be able to learn everything on your own, or you just want a more formal structure, you can join a course. Most courses are at your high school or community center, but you must understand that you will only do well on the test if you put in the effort. It's easy to slack off because there is not an actual grade for the course. Your "grade" is the actual score on the SAT exam. Do your homework religiously. Do not simply rely on the lectures to improve your scores. You must practice.

One-On-One Tutoring

At first glance, one-on-one tutoring can seem expensive, but the truth is high SAT or ACT scores make a huge difference in how much scholarship money you receive. You need to have a good score to get the money. Keep in mind that SAT or ACT tutoring should be used like any other kind of academic tutoring; the tutor is there to augment your knowledge not just spoon-feed it to you just because you paid them. Utilize them when you have a question or when you need something to be explained faster than you can study it yourself. It doesn't matter how high the tutor's SAT or ACT score was; you're the one taking the test. Your tutor is a great resource, but don't rely on them 100% to improve your score. Part of what you will be taught is how to approach the test and what concepts you need to know.

Chapter 32: The Big Lesson Gives You The Big Pay-Off!

"Education is transformational. It changes lives. That is why people work so hard to become educated."
— Condoleezza Rice

The next step you can take to get the money you need to pay for college is to find out your Expected Family Contribution (EFC), and then what steps you can take to yield a low EFC. Then you want to look at which schools will give your family the highest percent of need or the highest merit scholarships. Next, students should want to know what their chances are of getting into the desired colleges and what they can do to qualify. They must work to find out the application and financial aid deadlines for all the colleges under consideration. Finally, you can project your out-of-pocket college costs by visiting each school website and running a current Net Price Calculator. Then you can discuss with your family the best way to pay for the net costs.

To give your family the opportunity to pay for college on a wholesale basis, it all comes down to finding out and minimizing your Expected Family Contribution (EFC), and strategically applying to colleges that meet a high percent of need or provide the most generous merit scholarships.

If you want to save your retirement money, keep the equity you've built in your home, and maintain any of your other investments. Building a college funding plan can seem complicated. Don't let the complexities of the process stand in your way. After all, we are talking about tens of thousands of dollars that you can save and not have to pay. This is money you can use for retirement, to fund your business, or any of the many other expenses life brings your way.

But for now, let's focus on getting your children into the college that best suits who they are, and find ways to pay for it so you don't go broke or leave your students with $200,000 in student loans to pay off for the 10 to 25 years after college graduation.

You can avoid taking out loans, mortgaging your home, and liquidating your assets such as savings by following the path outlined to get what's available in scholarships and grants and use your knowledge to get your share of the free money without having to break the bank. Paying full price for your child to attend college is unnecessary, because there is a better way. You can get the schools to pay your child to attend.

The bottom line is that today's economy causes an uncertainty that we all face. It's really wise to pay as little money as possible for something as expensive as a college degree. Today, the cost of a college degree can easily run over $80,000 for a local college and over $280,000 for a private college or out–of-state university per child. So there's nothing wrong with doing this right and saving yourself $40,000 to $225,000 in college expenses to get your child a good education so they can have the best shot at life.

I want to thank you for taking the time to read this book, and I want you to know that I am a phone call away. If you have a student that wants to go to college and you don't want to pay full boat, you can call 626-657-7887 or go to www.collegefundingremedies.com to attend one of my workshops, webinars, or schedule a meeting with me so we can find out if I can be of service to you and determine what needs to be done to gain admission to the schools of your choice and get the money to pay for them.

About The Author

Trevor Ramos is a world-class scholarship and financial aid specialist. In just 6 years, he has helped over 200 families get their students accepted by the top colleges in America for pennies on the dollar by helping those students get free money grants and scholarships, over 12 million dollars!

Trevor's secret to success is successfully gained out of his own personal need. He was awarded $178,000 in financial aid by Boston University despite being told by counselors and coaches that community college was his best option. After his own personal achievements, he decided to devote his life and career to helping parents and students learn the truth about the college planning process and what it takes to get accepted to the college of your choice, receive thousands of dollars in scholarships and grants regardless of your income and assets, and pay for college without borrowing or using retirement money.

Made in the USA
San Bernardino, CA
27 September 2016